Poverty in America
Causes and Issues

Kathiann M. Kowalski

Enslow Publishers, Inc.

40 Industrial Road	PO Box 38
Box 398	Aldershot
Berkeley Heights, NJ 07922	Hants GU12 6BP
USA	UK

http://www.enslow.com

This book is dedicated to my son, Christopher Meissner.

Library of Congress Cataloging-in-Publication Data

Kowalski, Kathiann M., 1955–
    Poverty in America : causes and issues / Kathiann M. Kowalski.
        p. cm. — (Issues in focus)
    Summary: Explores the issues of poverty in the United States through real-life stories of poor people and the agencies and organizations available to help them.
    Includes bibliographical references and index.
    ISBN 0-7660-1945-4
    1. Poor—United States—Juvenile literature. 2. Poverty—United States—Juvenile literature. [1. Poor. 2. Poverty.] I. Title.
II. Series: Issues in focus (Hillside, N.J.)
HC110.P6 K63 2003
362.5'0973—dc21

                        2002156034

Printed in the United States of America

10 9 8 7 6 5 4 3 2 1

To Our Readers: We have done our best to make sure all Internet Addresses in this book were active and appropriate when we went to press. However, the author and the publisher have no control over and assume no liability for the material available on those Internet sites or on other Web sites they may link to. Any comments or suggestions can be sent by e-mail to comments@enslow.com or to the address on the back cover.

Illustration Credits: Courtesy of Ryan Beiler/Call to Renewal, pp. 60, 99; courtesy of Quinn Cassidy, pp. 8, 30; Corbis Images Royalty-Free, pp. 35, 55; DíAMAR Interactive Corp., p. 71; Dover Publications, p. 10; EyeWire Images, p. 93; Kathiann M. Kowalski, pp. 15, 76, 85, 106; Library of Congress, pp. 39, 44, 46, 48, 51, 53; Rubberball Productions, p. 89; U.S. Centers for Disease Control, p. 103; U.S. Department of Agriculture, pp. 26, 64; U.S. Department of Housing and Urban Development, p. 81.

Cover Illustrations: AP/Wide World. The photo shows a homeless family that walked across the United States for more than eighteen months before finding housing and employment in California.

Contents

Acknowledgments

The author thanks the following individuals and groups for sharing their comments and insights: Ryan Beiler and Marshela Salgado, Call to Renewal; Jill Duerr Berrick, Ph.D., University of California, Berkeley; Paul Campbell; Quinn K. Cassidy; Robert Haveman, Ph.D., University of Wisconsin-Madison; Mary Jane Sullivan, Massachusetts Coalition for the Homeless; James Weidman, The Heritage Foundation; Edward J. Welniak, Jr., Chief of the Income Surveys Branch, U.S. Census Bureau; Edward Wolff, Ph.D., New York University. Thanks too for the continuing love and support of my husband, Michael Meissner, and our children, Chris, Laura, and Bethany.

1

Unequal Wealth

Esther Iglesias wanted to give her four children a good home. She worked in Pennsylvania taking care of disabled children. The job was hard work, yet it provided money.

Then Iglesias had a car accident. Because of severe back pain, she had to quit her job. The family went to New York City. The children's father lived there, but he had no job. He could not house his children either.

Iglesias and her children went to a homeless shelter. Later, the Children's Aid Society got them a temporary place to stay in East Harlem. They got about $400 a month in welfare money. They also got food stamps worth another $300 a month. Medicaid would pay for medical costs.

The family still needed a permanent home. But it had limited options. "I'm so used to being a supportive parent," Iglesias told a *New York Times* reporter, "and I can't do that now."[1]

Many people would feel sympathetic toward Iglesias. No one wants to be hurt. No one wants to be homeless. Rather, most people want a good job. They want their children to have a nice home. They do not want to worry about money.

The case raises questions too. How poor was she? Could $300 a month stretch far enough to feed five people? It would depend on a family's food choices. Prime cuts of meat, fresh vegetables, and frozen convenience meals can make food costs soar. Menus planned around sales save money. More meatless meals help save too. Sodas, snack chips, and candy have little nutritional value. Skipping such items can also cut costs.

Could $400 a month cover everything else? Without more help, Iglesias probably could not pay for an apartment for her family. She could buy her children some clothes. Instead of $90 athletic shoes for her teenager daughter, she would probably have to choose $20 shoes.

The family had a roof over their heads. They could eat and buy some clothes. They could get medical care, schooling, and other services. But they could not have those things without government help.

Plus, they could not enjoy some things that many families take for granted. Meals at a sit-down family-style restaurant typically run $8 to $10 per person. Movie tickets cost around $8 for evening shows. Children's dance or swim lessons can cost over $50 per month.

How did the family get into its situation? The immediate cause was Iglesias's accident. Could she have gotten a job that did not involve physical labor?

Many jobs require a high school degree. A lot need a college degree too. Still other jobs use special skills, like keyboarding. If Iglesias did not have a good education, she would have fewer job choices.

The job market could limit her job choices too. Perhaps there were too few jobs in Pennsylvania and New York for the people who wanted them.

Iglesias's ex-husband raises more questions. Why did he not have a job? Most people would say that a father should help take care of his children.

People's values make them feel more or less sympathetic about why a parent might not have a job. Some may see the situation as a result of choices that an individual made throughout life. Other people may say someone is a victim of bad circumstances. Children complicate the matter. They have no choice over what family they get born into.

In short, families like Esther Iglesias's are in a difficult situation. As a factual matter, they have limited financial resources. As a result, they rely on government aid for various needs. Compared to the rest of America, they are poor.

While this girl's parents love her, poverty limits how much they can give her.

How people come to be poor is often a complex story. And how one responds to poverty depends on more than facts. In large part, it depends on people's values too.

The American Dream

As this century started, *Who Wants To Be a Millionaire?* ranked at the top of the TV ratings. Contestants vied for a chance to sit in the "hot seat." Then host Regis Philbin asked questions. A few lucky players survived every round. They became instant millionaires.

People can argue whether game show winners

deserve to be rich. Does knowledge of trivia and skill with a buzzer add any value to the economy? It does not make goods that people can use.

On the other hand, game shows entertain people, and they need contestants. Starring actors make millions for a single movie. Professional athletes make millions of dollars just for playing sports. Television, sports, and movies give other people jobs too. Thus, someone could argue that game show winners do something worthwhile. They provide entertainment.

What about the real world beyond game shows? The traditional "American dream" is that someone can do well if he or she has talent and works hard enough. This supposes that all people have a chance to better themselves. It also relies on a strong work ethic. In other words, people must take the initiative. They must work hard.

Can the American dream come true in real life? Many of America's richest people inherited their wealth. There is nothing wrong with being born rich. Indeed, the law lets people leave money and goods to whomever they want. But people lucky enough to be born rich did not have to work hard themselves to get there. They may also have more opportunities for a good education, quality health care, and other benefits. In short, many rich people got to be rich by routes other than the American dream.

A few "rags-to-riches" stories stand out. John Jacob Astor (1763–1848) rose from being a clerk to running America's biggest fur-trading company. He made more money by investing in land in Manhattan. Scottish immigrant Andrew Carnegie

(1835–1919) went from low-level jobs to owning the Carnegie Steel Company. By age sixty-five, Carnegie was the world's richest man. John D. Rockefeller (1839–1937) started out as a bookkeeper in Cleveland. He made a fortune in the oil business. Such stories are rare, though.

Yet many people have profited from hard work, education, and a will to succeed. Especially during the twentieth century, many Americans enjoyed upward mobility. They could move up from one socioeconomic level to another.

Julie grew up in a poor immigrant family. During the 1930s, her parents took care of a New York City apartment building. Neither went to school beyond eighth grade. Julie went to college, became a teacher, and married Ed. Ed's parents were also immigrants with limited income and education. Ed went to college after World War II and became a civil engineer. Together, Ed and Julie bought a house on Long Island and put six children through college.[2]

In 1900, Andrew Carnegie, the son of a Scottish weaver, was one of the world's richest men. He gave millions of dollars to various causes, such as libraries and schools.

Many other families were like Ed and Julie's. As children, the parents may have lived in poverty. Yet they valued hard work and education. They never went from "rags to riches." But their situation got better over time. They could give their children more than they had growing up.

Massachusetts Institute of Technology professor Frank Levy has linked rising income trends to changes in America's economy. World War II ended the Great Depression of the 1930s. But the war limited people's ability to buy new things. After the war, built-up demand led to a boom in new housing and consumer goods. Gains in productivity, or the ability to make things efficiently, led to more economic growth in the 1950s and early 1960s. By 1973, about two thirds of America's families had become part of the middle class.[3]

In this sense, many families have lived the American dream. "Mainstream" America offers opportunities. People can get a good education and use their talents to better their lot.

Today, however, some Americans feel left out of the American dream. They are not just poor. They have little hope of ever escaping poverty.

What Is Poverty?

Generally speaking, poverty is a lack of material resources. *Absolute poverty* means not having enough for a basic level of well-being. That includes a nutritious diet, housing, clothing, medical care, and other necessities.

Compared to other countries of the world, America has little absolute poverty. Some nations in Africa, Asia, and Latin America suffer widespread starvation, homelessness, infant mortality, and other problems.

Even a tiny percentage of people in absolute poverty matters, though. America has over 285 million people. As little as half a percent would still be over one million people. Plus, America is the world's richest country. With so many resources, why are so many people poor?

A second type of poverty is *relative poverty*. People living in relative poverty have enough to survive. Compared to most other people in their culture, however, they appear deprived.

A teenager may wear hand-me-down clothing. The family may not be able to afford new clothes, let alone brand-name sportswear or designer athletic shoes. If most other students have those items, the teenager may feel deprived. Likewise, a family may have a home, but it may be run-down or cramped.

People living in either absolute or relative poverty can feel powerless. They may feel unable to change their situation. That, in turn, can affect their sense of dignity and self-esteem.

Some poor people give up on the American dream. They live in an *underclass* culture. Basically, they are below or outside the social and economic system of "mainstream" America. They feel unable to move from one economic class to another.

Lack of money is not the only problem these people have. The Alan Guttmacher Institute says that over three fourths of teens who have babies come from poor and low-income families.[4] Susan Mayer at the University of Chicago found that in the poorest 20 percent of families, teens had a 34 percent risk of becoming high school dropouts. The middle 20 percent had less than half that risk.[5] Crime and other social ills also affect the poor more than other income groups.

Robert Rector of the Heritage Foundation feels that such "behavioral poverty" is a big reason why poverty is a persistent problem. He sees it as "a breakdown in the values and conduct that lead to the formation of healthy families, stable personalities, and self-sufficiency."[6] In his view, America must change poor people's behaviors and attitudes.

Other critics see poverty as a cause for different behaviors and attitudes in very poor communities. "In my view, these behaviors are due to the same causes that lead to nonmarital childbearing, etc., namely, growing up in poor dysfunctional families, lousy neighborhoods, and poor schools," says Robert Haveman at the University of Wisconsin-Madison. "Being a racial minority often decrees that one grows up in inner city neighborhoods with all of their problems. It is little wonder that people who grow up in such circumstances don't attain . . . success."[7]

Obviously, these are very different views. Some people see poverty as the result of individual values. Others feel that society as a whole bears responsibility.

Capitalism 101

Many people see America as a country of "haves" and "have-nots." How do the "haves" get what they've got? The answers lie in America's capitalist economy.

American capitalism is basically a free market system. Private persons or corporations own most businesses. If business is good, the people who own the business profit. For a corporation, those people are the shareholders.

Government interference in a free market system is limited. Some laws affect how people do business. Other laws deal with the money supply, interest rates, and other factors. Except for rare cases, like wartime, government does not say what people must charge for goods and services.

In contrast, in a socialist system, the government owns or runs big parts of the economy. Under communism, government ownership and management expand even more. Basically, the state owns all property and businesses. The state employs and pays all workers.

Whole books debate each system's merits. Each economic system has different goals. In theory, communism and socialism stress fairness and equality. In countries with a nationalized health system, for example, everyone gets the same level of medical care, regardless of the ability to pay. Communism aims to give workers control over the means of production. The state in theory represents all workers.

Many of America's middle-class and affluent teens enjoy frequent trips to the mall. Even if teens from low-income families live near malls, they may not be able to afford the latest fashion trends.

Capitalist theory says that free choice and competition are good for the economy. It assumes that people act in their own self-interest. It supposes that self-interest and fair competition will get people to allocate resources efficiently.

In general, the more demand there is for something, the more people will be willing to pay for it. That is especially true if supply is limited.

Look at the Furby. When the furry talking toy came out in 1998, many children wanted one. But there were not enough Furbies to go around. Shoppers lined up for hours at stores, hoping to buy one of the $30 toys. One woman got offers up to $750 from people who wanted to buy her spare Furby.

Demand is also a function of price. Few people could afford personal computers when they first came on the market. As prices came down, more people chose to spend their money for one. Now many middle-class families have a computer.

The profit motive should also affect job choices. Growth in an industry increases the need for skilled workers. As America's computer industry grew, for example, so did the need for computer engineers, factory workers, software writers, and so forth. Faced with a limited labor supply, competing employers will raise wages. Good wages will attract people to a field. The labor supply will increase.

Competition should cause movement toward equilibrium, or a balance. That is, the level of production should make the most profit for companies based on how much consumers are willing to pay.

Wages for jobs should reflect the value of work that goes into goods or services and their relative value to the overall economy.

In theory, capitalism should maximize benefits for everyone. "Maximize" does not mean that everyone gets a lot. Instead, the market should use its resources in the most efficient way. Competition should produce the blend of goods and services that best matches informed buyers' ability and willingness to pay at that time.

Of course, each type of economic system rests on value judgments. Plus, theory and real life are two different things. The real world is not always efficient.

Resources cannot always move from one area to another. Someone who loses one job cannot always get other work. Other jobs may need different skills. Or, they may require that a person move to a new area.

Often factors limit competition. By law, companies must pay at least minimum wage for most jobs. The law protects workers, but it adds to companies' costs. Companies may be able to accept a lower profit. Or they may raise prices for consumers.

Patents also limit competition. A patent gives an inventor the sole right to decide who makes an invention for a limited time. During that time, patent holders can charge higher prices.

Taxes affect the market too. Tax benefits can make some investments more attractive than others. Tax burdens can decrease demand for other items.

Tastes change too. Sometimes people's lifestyles

change over time. Other times, advertising shapes people's tastes. In any case, business slows down in some parts of the market. Other parts of the market pick up.

The economy is a dynamic, or changing, system. The balance of supply and demand changes over time. Generally, such changes can trigger other effects throughout the economy.

The Income Gap

In 2000, the median income for American households before taxes was $42,148. "Half have incomes above that number and half below," explains Edward Welniak, Jr., at the U.S. Census Bureau.[8]

But income is not distributed evenly. *Income inequality* describes how income is spread out among the population. Journalists also call it the *income gap*.

The Gini index of income inequality ranges from one to zero. "Zero means perfect equality. Everyone shares equally in the wealth," says Welniak. "One means perfect inequality—one person has everything and everybody else has nothing."[9]

The actual numbers are somewhere in between. From 1967 to 1975, the Gini index ranged from 0.394 to 0.399. Income inequality rose after that until the 1990s. By 2000, the Gini index was 0.460.[10] The higher number means more inequality.

Another approach is to compare groups. In 2000, about 5 percent of households earned over $145,000. About 10 percent earned less than $10,600.

That same year, the top quintile of households earned almost half of all household income. A quintile is 20 percent of the values, ranked in order. The top quintile is the one fifth of households earning the most money. The lowest quintile is the one fifth of households making the least money.

"The analogy would be a piece of pie," says Welniak. "You would cut the pie into five equal pieces if everyone shared equally." But that is not the case. "One group gets almost half, while the others get progressively less." Thus, as shown on the chart on the next page, the highest quintile, or fifth, had 49.7 percent of all household income in 2000. The next highest quintile earned 23.0 percent. The middle fifth got 14.8 percent. The second lowest had 9.0 percent. The bottom group earned only 3.6 percent of all income.[11]

If everyone's real income goes up, income equality is not a problem. (Real income numbers factor out inflation.) Think of how a rising tide lifts all boats at a dock. As a whole, Americans fare far better today than they did in the 1930s. If some groups' real income goes down, however, that can be a problem.

"People with low skills have experienced falling real wages since the early 1980s," notes economist Robert Haveman at the University of Wisconsin-Madison. "This growing earnings inequality has led to falling income and increased poverty."[12]

Again, values affect how people view the income gap. Traditionally, Americans value equality. The income gap seems unfair if people think the top earners prosper at other people's expense.

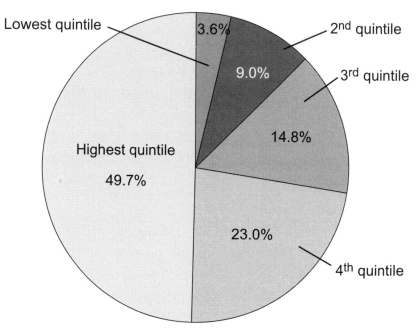

Income Distribution by Quintile: 2000

Source: U.S. Census Bureau, Money Income in the United States: 2000.

In 2001, for example, America's top corporate executives earned over five hundred times the average worker's salary. Were top executives really worth their average $13.1 million annual pay?[13] Labor unions like the AFL-CIO argue that executives do not deserve so much money. After all, unions want more money and better working conditions for members.

Americans also pride themselves on caring about people. People feel pity when they read about a homeless person freezing to death on a cold night. They feel bad about children who grow up in poor neighborhoods. In a land where some people have so much, people may ask, is it fair that other people have so little?

On the other hand, Americans reward hard work and self-reliance. Why shouldn't people make as much money as they can? Suppose someone in the top quintile went to college and works sixty hours a week in a high-pressure job. Suppose someone in the bottom quintile dropped out of school and has no job. Is it fair to compare the two?

Americans want value for their money. A big company's top executive has a lot of responsibility. His or her judgment affects shareholders' profits. It also influences the company's ability to stay in business and pay its workers. Why shouldn't companies pay top dollar for someone who adds value to the business?

Americans also prize creativity. Sometimes businesspeople come up with a new product or idea at just the right time. That can enable a company to make huge profits. Why shouldn't the people involved be rewarded?

"The freedom to turn thoughts, hunches, insights and dreams into realities not only makes America rich but also keeps it perpetually on the move, open to new things and to new ways of doing things," wrote Steve Forbes, owner of *Forbes Magazine*.[14] Each year the magazine makes its list of America's four hundred wealthiest people. Various people on recent years' lists made their fortunes by being early leaders in their industry. Microsoft founder Bill Gates is a good example.

Innovations—new ways of doing things—can make life better for everyone. The pioneering industry leaders profit. Society profits too. It gets a better way to do something. Plus, innovation creates new job opportunities.

"We have demonstrated, as no other economy has," says Forbes, "that life need not be a zero-sum game, that one person's gain is not necessarily another person's loss."[15] In other words, economics is not a winner-take-all situation. People can profit at the top of the income scale. But it need not be at the expense of other people. If the economy grows, people at the bottom levels can do better too. Viewed this way, the income gap is not in itself unfair. It shows (although imperfectly) how society values people's contributions.

Overall, America has one of the world's highest standards of living. Yet, says the Census Bureau, about 30 million people live in poverty. The economic system distributes wealth in America. Whether it does so fairly depends on one's values. As you read this book, think about how your values affect your views on poverty.

2

Who Are the Poor?

What do you think of when you hear the word "poverty"? Pictures painted by media reports often show the poor in "standard" ways. One image shows a never-married, unemployed mother and her children in a ghetto. Another image shows an unemployed alcoholic.

Neither view is very sympathetic. Nor is either stereotype (preset notion) really accurate. In reality, poverty has many faces. Poverty plagues a homeless man sleeping under a bridge. Poverty surrounds a single mother and her children in a tiny apartment. Poverty affects a family

23

in a run-down farmhouse. Poverty haunts an elderly person on a limited income. Persons of color are poor, as well as white people. In short, poor people are a mixed group.

This chapter looks at poverty statistics. It examines poor people's varied situations. Faces of poverty differ. Yet all people deserve dignity and respect.

How Poor Is Poor?

Gauging the extent of poverty is hard. Just how much money is "enough"?

"If you view people who are at the bottom of the nation's income distribution as being poor, there will always be folks at the bottom," notes Robert Haveman at the University of Wisconsin-Madison. "We, in the U.S., measure poverty by comparing the annual income of a family to an absolute standard, which depends on the families' size."[1] These standards are the *poverty thresholds*.

Mollie Orshansky at the Social Security Administration first developed the poverty thresholds in 1963–1964. "If it is not possible to state unequivocally 'how much is enough,'" Orshansky wrote, "it should be possible to assert with confidence how much, on an average, is too little."[2] The Department of Agriculture had said about one third of families' after-tax income went for food. It also published four food plans. Each plan gave adequate nutrition at different spending levels. (Of course, no one had to follow any particular food plan.)

Orshansky figured out costs for the cheapest food

plan. In theory, food was one third of families' spending. If a family had money problems, it would likely cut back in other areas too. Thus, Orshansky multiplied by three to get poverty thresholds. In 1963, the cheapest food plan for a non-farm family of four cost about $1,043 annually. Thus, the poverty threshold for such a family was $3,130.[3]

For a while, the government recalculated the poverty thresholds each year. After 1967, it just adjusted the numbers for inflation. The government changed the method a bit in later years.

Family size, age, and number of children all affect the poverty thresholds. As of 2002, the Census Bureau used forty-eight poverty thresholds. In 2000, the average poverty threshold for a four-person family was $17,603. For one person, it was $8,794. For nine people or more, the number was $35,060.[4]

The poverty thresholds may overestimate poverty. For one thing, they do not count all government aid. With that money, families can spend more. Thus, poor households are not as deprived as the dollar numbers suggest.

Consumption—how much people spend for goods and services—might be a better way to measure financial well-being. The Consumer Expenditure Survey by the Census Bureau and the Bureau of Labor Statistics reports on Americans' spending. While those numbers are good, however, they are not as complete as income data. It is also hard to say how much total wealth everyone has in America. Is someone who spends a lot really richer than someone who saves money?

The Social Security Administration developed different food plans and calculated poverty thresholds based on them.

Other arguments can show that the poverty thresholds are too low. The Census Bureau only has reliable data on pre-tax income. It uses those numbers to figure poverty rates. But families can only spend after-tax dollars. The Census Bureau also does not adjust for medical or other special needs.

The poverty thresholds are also somewhat arbitrary. They assume that one third of a family's income goes for food. But people spend their money in many different ways.

Plus, expenses do not go up at the same rate. In general, housing costs have risen faster than food costs. In some areas, rents have skyrocketed. Families making the same amount of money may have different levels of poverty based on where they live.

The poverty thresholds are not perfect. On the other hand, they are a standard measure. Having a common yardstick helps.

The government has looked at other ways to measure poverty. Social services agencies, for example, use different guidelines to say who gets benefits. Such guidelines are often more generous than the poverty thresholds. For measuring poverty in America, though, the Census Bureau still uses the poverty thresholds. Unless otherwise noted, this book uses those figures too.

Poverty by the Numbers

Census Bureau statistics are numerical pictures of the American people. As of 2000, the poverty rate was 11.3 percent. This was not statistically different from 1973's record-low rate of 11.1 percent. That was the good news.

The bad news was that 31.1 million people lived in poverty during 2000—over 8 million more than the number in 1973. Over 11 million poor people in 2000 were children under age eighteen. More than 3 million were people over age sixty-five.[5]

Poverty affects ethnic groups differently. The 2000 poverty rate for African Americans was 22.1 percent. For Hispanics of all races, it was 21.2 percent. Both these figures were record lows. Yet the poverty rate for Asian and Pacific Islanders was 10.8 percent.

The poverty rate for white non-Hispanics was only 7.5 percent.[6]

Poverty rates can and do change. Economic growth can lower poverty rates. More people can get jobs. Companies can afford to pay more too. On the other hand, economic downturns can raise poverty rates. When business is bad, people lose jobs.

Metropolitan Poverty

Most of America's population lives in cities and suburbs. Thus, most poor people live in metropolitan areas too. In 2000, over 24 million people below the poverty thresholds lived in metropolitan areas. That was 78 percent of the total. About 40 percent of America's poor people live in central cities.[7]

The Census Bureau says a central city is the largest one or two places in a metropolitan area. Cities have different neighborhoods. Housing in poor neighborhoods is older but costs less. Public transportation is often available too. People without cars need that.

Yet people pay other costs for living in poor neighborhoods. Lower property values mean less money gets paid for property taxes. Property taxes are a major source of school funding in most of the United States. Thus, many central city schools are short on funds.

Joblessness plagues many central cities too. Since World War II, many companies have moved to other parts of the country or overseas, where labor costs less. That has meant fewer jobs for low-skilled workers.

In *When Work Disappears*, William Julius Wilson argues that joblessness leads to inner-city poverty. That triggers family breakups, crime, substance abuse, and other ills. Ghettos attract few jobs, so the problem feeds on itself.[8]

Because of higher crime rates, businesses in poor neighborhoods have higher security costs. They raise prices to cover those costs. They may also raise prices if neighborhood people have nowhere else to buy groceries or other basics. Thus, central-city poor people pay more than they would if they lived in suburbs and had cars.

Poverty is less visible in areas outside the central city, but it is no less real. In one northern Ohio suburb, a family could not buy its teen daughter a winter coat. Another parent could not buy eyeglasses for her son. Another family could not pay its overdue electric bill.[9]

Yet the same suburb has hundreds of nice four-bedroom homes. It even has small mansions near a scenic valley. Residents include doctors, lawyers, professors, engineers, and other well-paid professionals. Even in middle-class towns, poverty can be a problem.

Rural Poverty

America's rural areas are incredibly beautiful. Yet about one in five poor Americans lives in the countryside—almost 7 million people.[10]

The "James" family (not their real name) in rural South Carolina is one example. Mr. James works full time, but his factory wages are low. Mrs. James cares for their children. Their ages range from preschool through elementary school.

Instead of a regular house, the James family lives in a trailer with a room built on to it. The trailer sits on land that the family got from relatives. Until a few years ago, the James home had no running water. The family used an outhouse instead of a bathroom. They drank unpurified water from a stream.

As a summer project, volunteers from a youth group built a system to bring clean running water to the home. The group also cleared a lot of debris around the home. In most middle-class neighborhoods, people never leave litter around. But people

Volunteers from a youth organization helped the low-income family living in this home in rural South Carolina.

in rural areas must often cart trash to a landfill. Sometimes they have to pay to throw their trash away there.

"At times it was disgusting, but mostly it was just very, very sad," says one volunteer. "I ached for this family, because I saw no way in which they could pull themselves up out of their poverty with the double whammy of economics and society."[11] As she saw it, the father had a low-paying job. One of the children was sick a lot. All the children did poorly in school.

Prospects for the rural poor look bleak. Since the 1950s, mining and other industries have scaled back in rural areas. New businesses have generally gone near metropolitan areas instead. Businesses that stayed need not pay a lot to compete for workers without special skills.

Why do people like the James family stay? For one thing, it is their home. They have family and friends nearby. Plus, moving would cost money and mean lost work time. And there is no guarantee that things would be better elsewhere.

Working Poor

Gabriella Corona made $7.25 an hour at her food service job. That was still too little for rent, food, clothing, and day care. With four young children, Corona had no time to go to college either. It seemed like she would work forever at low-wage jobs.[12]

Often, even single people cannot support themselves adequately. Journalist Barbara Ehrenreich chose to find this out firsthand. From 1998 to 2000, she got jobs as a waitress, maid, nursing home aide, and department store salesclerk. *Nickel and Dimed: On (Not) Getting By in America* tells her story.[13]

All Ehrenreich's jobs paid more than minimum wage. All involved exhausting work. None of the jobs paid enough for a nutritious diet, a comfortable home, nice clothing, transportation, and medical care.

Ehrenreich could go home when she got too broke or too tired. Her coworkers did not have that choice. One person lived out of a car. Other people packed into cramped quarters with friends. Still others lived in cheap hotels. They had no down payment for an apartment.

Even with two or three jobs, getting by on low-wage work is tough. Plus, it is physically and mentally exhausting. Without a good education, many people have no other options. Most healthy people without children cannot get long-term government help, either.

Single Mothers

Sandy got pregnant during her first year of college. She and the father did not marry, so Sandy became a single mother. She worked part-time for a while, until her baby got an ear infection. Because her job had no medical benefits, Sandy quit and went on welfare. She got Medicaid to pay for the doctor's bills. Some critics might say Sandy took advantage of the system. Sandy felt she had to do that for her child.[14]

Over one in four American children lives with

a single parent. Some parents have never married. Others are divorced.

Compared to those in two-parent homes, children who live with a single parent are more likely to be poor. According to a 1997 Census Bureau study, "About 45 percent of children raised by divorced mothers and 69 percent of those raised by never-married mothers lived in or near poverty."[15]

Employment was one factor. Many single mothers work. But despite civil rights laws, men as a group still earn more in America than women do.

Beyond this, never-married mothers were twice as likely as divorced mothers to have no job. With no job, they had to rely on government help or child support. Laws in every state call for parents to pay child support, but some fathers cannot or will not pay it.

Education plays a role too. The Census Bureau said less than two thirds of never-married mothers had finished high school. Even if they got a job, it was more likely to be low paying.

People can debate about whether or not single parenthood is a choice. They can also argue that both parents should take care of their children's needs. Meanwhile, nearly six in ten children living with a single mother grow up poor.

Struck by Sickness

Esther Iglesias in Chapter 1 "got by" until her accident. Because she was hurt, she lost her job. Her family became homeless.

David in Washington, D.C., likewise became

homeless after he developed heart problems. He could not work while he was sick. By the time he got better, the medical bills had piled up.[16]

Health insurance can limit medical costs. People pay money to an insurance company. The company then pays for doctors, hospital stays, or other covered expenses.

But insurance costs money. The average plan for a family of four costs over $7,000 per year. Sometimes employers pay part of this cost. Other times, people pay it all themselves.[17]

Families USA is a health-care consumers group. It says over 13 million adults nationwide lack medical insurance. They cannot get public help with medical costs either, even with incomes twice as high as the poverty thresholds.

"For uninsured low-income adults, the health care safety net is wholly inadequate," announced Families USA Executive Director Ron Pollack. "Many millions of low-wage, working adults, who don't have employer health coverage and who can't afford to buy coverage, are left unprotected by public health programs in their states."[18]

Addiction and Other Mental Illness

Joann drank heavily and used crack cocaine. Unable to hold down a job, she lost her home in Washington, D.C. Once someone beat her badly. Another person raped Joann at a homeless shelter. Joann ended up in a hospital psychiatric unit. Finally, she got treatment for her drug addiction.[19]

Illness and injury can make it hard for people to keep their jobs and stay out of poverty.

Joann's addiction caused her poverty and homelessness. Often children also suffer because of parents' addictions. Either way, substance abuse keeps people from holding a steady job. It eats up money that should pay for food, shelter, and medical expenses.

Other mental illness leads to poverty too. "Stan" (not his real name) had schizophrenia. The mental illness made him hear voices and act irrationally. Because he could not hold a steady job, Stan became homeless.

Psychiatric treatment can help Stan and other mentally ill persons. Sadly, many communities do not have good mental health services for poor people. Without government help, people may be unable to pay for medicines. Also, certain medicines have bad side effects. To avoid them, some patients skip the medicine.

"Poverty is one of the more unfortunate, yet silent, symptoms of mental illness," says the National Alliance for the Mentally Ill. The group says between 85 and 90 percent of people with severe mental illness are unemployed.[20] About one third of the nation's homeless population has a treatable severe mental illness.[21]

Always on the Move

Fourteen-year-old Jose was one of about 150,000 children working on farms in the United States. For just $160 a week, he picked fruits and vegetables in the hot sun. Jose was a migrant worker.[22]

Migrant workers take work wherever they can get it. Many labor up to 70 hours a week. They get no overtime pay. They also get no pay for months they do not work. For all this, each migrant worker makes an average of just $7,500 a year. That places almost all migrant workers below the poverty thresholds.[23]

Why would people take such jobs? Some do it because their families have done farm work for a long time. Some speak little or no English. Others have no skills for other jobs.

Most migrant workers are in the United States lawfully. But some are illegal aliens. If farm owners hire them illegally, they may take advantage of them. This raises ethical and legal problems. Should farm owners just have illegal aliens arrested instead of giving them jobs? Or should farm owners pay all workers fairly whether they are in the country legally or not?

Old and Poor

Programs such as Social Security and Medicare provide a "safety net" that saves most elderly people from poverty. Yet one in ten elderly people still fell below the poverty thresholds in 2000.

Many elderly people rely on a fixed income. A fixed income basically stays the same over time. Meanwhile, rents, utility bills, food costs, and other expenses may go up.

As a group, older people face higher medical costs too. Medicare covers some expenses. Yet prescriptions remain a big problem.

Families USA says the average elderly person's prescription costs will rise from about $1,200 in 2000 to over $2,800 in 2010. "Older Americans live on fixed incomes, like Social Security and pensions, and yet the prices of their prescriptions are skyrocketing," said Ron Pollack of Families USA. "These price increases cannot be justified and are making prescription medicines unaffordable for too many seniors."[24] Whether drug prices are too high is open to debate. Drug companies say the prices reflect high research and marketing expenses.

In any case, prices are a problem if people cannot get medicine. During the 2000 election campaign, both Democrats and Republicans promised a prescription drug plan for seniors. At the end of 2002, however, Congress had not passed a drug plan law.

Costs of Poverty

Obviously, poverty causes problems for poor people. By definition, people suffering absolute poverty cannot pay for basic needs. They may not eat an adequate diet. They may lack decent clothing. They may live in substandard housing. They may forgo medical care.

The income gap is about more than money. People raised in poverty are more apt to fall short on several scales. Ultimately, that affects society.

Poor children suffer higher health risks. Poor parents cannot pay for good medical care. They may also know less about how to spot symptoms or prevent illness. Pest infestation, bad ventilation, peeling lead-based paint, and other problems add to illness too.

Poor children tend to score lower on math and reading achievement tests than other children. The causes are not clear. Serious deprivation can keep children from concentrating on studies. Schools may lack enough money to provide a good education. Children in poor families are less likely to have parents who spend time reading to them. They often miss out on music lessons, sports, and other activities too.

Schools in many poor neighborhoods have high rates of absenteeism. Parents may worry whether schools are safe. Some parents work odd hours and have trouble getting children to school. Or parents may just not place a high priority on getting children to school. The stress of poverty may distract parents from supporting children's efforts to learn. Or parents may not know how to help their children.

Problems plague poor teenagers too. In one study, girls from the poorest 20 percent of families were eight times more likely to become

Migrant workers have followed the crops all over America, working for low pay in poor conditions. This girl was picking strawberries in Louisiana in 1939.

teen mothers than girls from high-income families. Poor teens were also five times more likely to drop out of high school.[25]

By adulthood, people from poor families generally earn less than those from better-off families. In one study, young adult males from the poorest quintile of families earned 32 percent less, on average, than young men from the richest quintile. Young adults from poor families were twice as likely to be on welfare than those from the middle quintile income range.[26] Education, skills, and personal goals all play a role.

Does more money make the problems go away? Susan E. Mayer at the University of Chicago studied what happens as family income goes up a little for poor families. Parents do spend more on children for certain basic needs. After that, parents did not automatically spend extra income on children. That money might go for entertainment, nicer furniture, or other things parents wanted. Extra income had some effect on poor children's outcomes. But money alone did not explain all the differences between rich and poor children.[27]

When people do not achieve as much as they could, society as a whole loses out. School districts pay more if poor children must repeat a grade. Businesses lose out when there is a smaller talent pool of skilled labor. Taxpayers ultimately bear the burden for higher health care, criminal justice, social services, and other costs linked to poverty. Poor people generally have a lower life expectancy too.

All these costs add up. The Children's Defense

Fund claims that America's economy loses $130 billion for each year that 14.5 million children remain poor.[28]

Yet dollars cannot count all the human and social costs of poverty. How much better would society be if a lack of money did not stop people from reaching their potential?

3

What Has America Done About Poverty?

Poverty in America is nothing new. Yet America's population has grown dramatically. By 2000, over 280 million people lived in America. Even a "low" poverty rate of 11.3 percent affects over 31 million people.

America started out as a rural society. Now most Americans live in cities and suburbs. With so many people living closely together, poverty is more obvious. As America has changed, so has its approach to poverty.

The Nineteenth Century: Deserving vs. Undeserving Poor

From America's earliest times, people's view of the poor has often been based on whether they were "deserving" or "undeserving." "Deserving poor" people were in circumstances beyond their control. Orphaned or abandoned children were seen as deserving. So were widowed or abandoned women, as well as elderly and disabled people. Many people felt a religious duty to help these people.

In contrast, most people believed that healthy people should work. Men without jobs seemed lazy or sinful. They were the "undeserving poor." Giving money to such people would reward laziness, people thought. Many Americans still have a strong work ethic. They still feel handouts are wrong. But even with a job, people could not always support their families well.

Early America treated the problem of poverty on a local level. Some churches and communities gave "outdoor relief." This did not mean campouts for the poor. Rather, it was help outside the doors of institutions. People got food and some money for most basic needs.

By the mid-nineteenth century, America had more almshouses, or poorhouses. They housed both adults and children. Mentally ill people often went there too. The poorhouses kept many people from starving. But few people thrived there.

Later, orphan asylums, or orphanages, housed just children. Many children's parents had died.

Other children had parents who could not afford to care for them. Living in an orphanage was better than starving. The orphan asylums also got children away from mentally ill people in poorhouses. But most orphanages gave neither a good education nor loving care.

Even outside such places, many people were poor compared to today's standards. Near cities, factory wages were low. Work was often dangerous too. Sometimes accidents happened. Then families were often left with nothing.

Orphanages house children whose parents have died or who cannot take care of them for other reasons. Shown are children in an orphanage in 1918.

Some rural farmers did well. Others barely eked out a living. A poor harvest could wipe out a family's income.

After the Civil War, the South's economy was in ruins. Former slaves were free. Many had no choice but to work as sharecroppers for former slave owners. Many poor white people became sharecroppers too. Sharecroppers farmed someone else's land, but they got only a small share of the harvest—too little to support a family properly.

New Ideas and New Laws

By the end of the nineteenth century, labor reformers sought safer work conditions and better pay. They wanted government to regulate business. Yet reforms like minimum wage laws were still decades away.

Meanwhile, William Graham Sumner (1840–1910) and Herbert Spencer (1820–1903) talked about Social Darwinism. In science, Charles Darwin had said that evolution depends on survival of the fittest. Sumner and Spencer argued that this applied to society too. If rich people were "fit," then poor people were "unfit." Government should not interfere, they said.

Sociologist Lester Frank Ward (1841–1913) took the opposite view. He felt that strong people needed restraints. Otherwise, they would take advantage of weaker groups. Ward and other reformers wanted government to protect people.

During the Progressive Era of 1900–1914, America adopted new child welfare laws, plus early

Labor reforms in the early part of the twentieth century aimed to end child labor as well as improve conditions for other workers. Here a fifteen-year old girl is working in a cotton mill in Massachusetts in 1916.

health and safety laws. Limited unemployment and disability protections helped too.

World War I came. The Roaring Twenties followed. America still had poor people. And many Americans felt that poverty came from poor moral character. The federal government avoided the issue. But that was about to change.

The Great Depression

The Roaring Twenties came to a screeching halt on October 24, 1929, with New York's stock market crash. People had speculated wildly in the stock market. But the prices did not reflect real value. Suddenly, stock prices came tumbling down. Many people lost their life's savings.

Just a year earlier, President Herbert Hoover had promised, "A chicken in every pot and a car in every garage."[1] Now companies were going bankrupt. Unemployment skyrocketed.

By the early 1930s, one in four workers had lost their jobs. In the cities, soup kitchen lines snaked out the doors. Former businessmen would do any odd job for cash.

Many families broke apart under the stress. Others stayed together but lost their homes. Shantytowns, made of shacks built from packing crates and sheet metal scraps, sprung up around cities.

People in rural areas suffered too. Unable to pay the mortgage, many people lost their farms. The Dust Bowl of the 1930s made matters worse. Drought combined with poor soil care practices to destroy harvests across the Great Plains.

Some people left their farms to join job seekers in cities. Others turned to sharecropping. Still others went west and became migrant workers.

Now poverty was almost everywhere. For the first time, most Americans did not see poverty as mainly a character flaw. Clearly, the economy played a role.

Private charities could not handle the widespread poverty of the Great Depression. State and local governments were helpless too. Americans wanted the federal government to act.

Elected in 1932 to his first of four terms,

During the Great Depression, millions of people were out of work. Many were reduced to selling apples, like this unemployed man in front of the U.S. capitol building in Washington, D.C.

President Franklin Roosevelt promised Americans a "New Deal." "The only thing we have to fear is fear itself," he said.[2]

New Deal programs got government into poverty relief in a big way. The Federal Emergency Relief Administration gave money for the most needy people.

The Social Security Act of 1935 set up a "safety net" for vulnerable groups. Workers and employers would pay a percentage of salaries to the Social Security Administration. When people reached age sixty-five, workers would get back money. It was like a forced savings plan. Widowed and disabled people could also get money from the Social Security Administration.

Social Security payments have never been big. Yet many older people rely on them. Without their monthly checks, it is estimated that 60 percent of unmarried elderly people would be poor.[3]

The Social Security Act also set up a federal program for poor children. It gave money to states to help widowed or deserted mothers raise their families. Later the program came to be known as Aid to Families with Dependent Children (AFDC). Over time, more AFDC money went to never-married mothers. Even later, it helped married couples with children too. Often people referred to AFDC simply as "welfare."

The New Deal did not just hand out money. It also created jobs. Young men in the Civilian Conservation Corps worked on flood control, parks, and other public projects. The Works Progress

Administration built hospitals, schools, and libraries. Taxes ultimately paid for these programs.

Other laws regulated businesses. Starting in 1938, covered workers got a minimum wage—$.25 per hour. That was worth about $3.05 in 2000 dollars.[4]

The New Deal programs helped millions of people survive extreme poverty. Beyond this, the New Deal greatly expanded the federal government's role in social welfare programs.

World War II finally lifted America out of the Great Depression. The war created a huge demand for equipment, supplies, and soldiers. That put people back to work. Many items were in short supply. But people could at least buy food and clothing again.

The "Other America"

America's economy boomed after World War II. Once again, people could buy consumer goods. People wanted new homes too, so suburbs sprang up around cities. Veterans' benefits sent many former soldiers to college. The degrees helped them get good jobs.

But the postwar prosperity had limits. People who did well were mostly white families headed by men. Others often fell behind.

Before the 1960s civil rights era, racial discrimination was common. Bias was based on gender, age, and religion too. Bigotry denied many people jobs. It made others take lower pay. Prejudice also limited educational choices.

Meanwhile, many central cities lost jobs. Some

companies moved somewhere else in the United States. Others had unskilled work done cheaper overseas. Central cities' ghettos grew.

Rural areas struggled too. Appalachia is one of America's poorest rural areas. It stretches along the Appalachian Mountains from Pennsylvania to northern Georgia. Until the 1960s, strip mining ripped coal and valuable topsoil from the surface. Lumber workers clear-cut trees but often did not plant new ones. Those practices destroyed land and resources. As job opportunities dwindled, poverty grew.

Many Americans took an "out of sight, out of mind" attitude about the poor. Then, in 1962, author Michael Harrington published *The Other America*. Poverty, he argued, had become largely "invisible" as middle-class Americans moved to the suburbs. They did not see the squalor of city slums. They did not see bleak poverty in America's rural areas. Yet one in four Americans—between 40 and 50 million people—were poor.[5]

In the rural south, areas of poverty persisted throughout the twentieth century. Shown is a boy on a cotton farm on the Mississippi Delta in 1940.

Millions of people in the "other America" seemed stuck in a vicious cycle. The problem was not just money. Fathers who had lost their jobs lost status. "Street smarts"—the ability to survive on the streets—became more important than "school smarts." Changes in family structure, education, and attitudes added up to a "culture of poverty."

Lyndon Johnson became president after John F. Kennedy was killed in November 1963. In 1964, Johnson declared an "unconditional war on poverty in America."[6] His "Great Society" programs dealt with poverty, discrimination, cities, and other issues.

The Job Corps gave young adult dropouts skills to get jobs. Project Head Start ran preschool programs to get poor children ready for school. The food stamp program helped poor people buy food. All these programs continue today.

The Medicare and Medicaid programs were started in 1965. Medicare is basic health insurance for elderly people. Medicaid is a state-run program. Medicaid pays basic medical costs for poor people. The federal government matches a share of states' money. Funding and benefits vary from state to state. Most Medicaid recipients are poor families with children. Low-income elderly and disabled people can get help too. Very few states let healthy, childless people get Medicaid.

The Johnson administration also set up the Department of Housing and Urban Development. Early "housing projects" built during the 1950s and 1960s were often huge apartment complexes. HUD made it easier for very poor people to get into public housing run by local authorities. But as the percentage of working people living in some projects went down, crime, drugs, and gangs became serious problems.

Urban renewal aimed to attract new businesses to cities. But only a fraction of new jobs went to low-skilled workers. Meanwhile, developers often tore down older buildings where poor people lived and put up new buildings with much higher rents. The low-rent housing supply dropped.

During the 1960s, Congress passed new civil rights laws. Court decisions also struck down discrimination. These legal changes gave more opportunities to women and minorities.

Growth of the "Welfare State"

The welfare program grew dramatically after Johnson became president. In 1960, 3.1 million people received AFDC. That number nearly doubled to 6.1 million by 1969. By 1974, the figure was 10.8 million. By 1996, nearly five times that many got welfare.[7]

President Lyndon Johnson set up a number of programs to aid the poor in what he called the War on Poverty.

Before the 1960s, state social workers often used "moral standards" to deny AFDC to persons of color. They denied help to many never-married mothers too. Legal changes in the 1960s broke down those barriers. From 1972 to 1992, says Susan Mayer at the University of Chicago, welfare rolls mostly mirrored population growth.[8]

Bigger welfare rolls meant more spending. But that spending did not end poverty. Poverty rates dropped from around 25 percent in 1962 to 11.1 percent in 1973. After that, poverty rates varied. 1983 and 1993 saw rates over 15 percent.[9]

Welfare's costs bred resentment. Why should taxpayers support a program that did not succeed in reducing poverty? Indeed, critics challenged, why weren't welfare recipients working?

Also, critics noted, single women headed many welfare families. Where were the fathers? Shouldn't they support their own children?

Yet if welfare parents got jobs, their benefits went down somewhat. Many parents did not report all income. That led to feelings that welfare fueled fraud.

The 1988 Family Support Act dealt with some issues. It got more child support from fathers. It started a limited job-training program. It called for states to help more two-parent families too.

Changing Welfare "As We Know It"

Despite the 1988 changes, the welfare system still had problems. Job training and education were good ideas, but only a small share of welfare recipients got them. Meanwhile, welfare rolls remained high.

Media reports of abuse fueled the fire. In Illinois, forty-three-year-old Theresa Henderson allegedly stole over $350,000 in welfare money and food stamps. She had allegedly made up five fake families with twenty-seven nonexistent children. In New York, police said that sixty-three-year-old Herbert Steed had collected welfare while owning three cars and renting a posh apartment. Another New York woman allegedly used fifteen aliases to get over $400,000 for over six dozen fake children.[10]

Critics hated that welfare was a handout. They said that people had stopped relying on their own efforts and had come to depend on welfare.

Welfare also came under attack for weakening American families. A 1996 Congressional report cited a 400 percent increase in out-of-wedlock births since the 1950s. Indeed, welfare families could often do better if the father did not live

Most parents help their children with schoolwork and support their efforts to learn. Parents in poor families are not always able to do this.

with the mother and children. It was easier to get money with only one income. The report said:

> There is little doubt that the current welfare system is a failure. It traps recipients in a cycle of dependency. It undermines the values of work and family that form the foundation of America's communities. . . .
>
> The welfare system contradicts fundamental American values that ought to be encouraged and rewarded: work, family, personal responsibility, and self-sufficiency. Instead, the system subsidizes dysfunctional behavior.[11]

During his 1992 campaign, Democratic President Bill Clinton vowed to "end welfare as we know it."[12] Republicans promised welfare reform too in their 1994 Contract with America. Republicans won control of both houses of Congress in 1994.

In 1996, Congress passed the Personal Responsibility and Work Opportunity Reconciliation Act. President Clinton praised this as "real welfare reform," saying, "The current welfare system is fundamentally broken, and this may be our last best chance to set it straight."[13]

The law got rid of AFDC. No longer would welfare be an *entitlement*—something people got as a matter of right. TANF—Temporary Aid for Needy Families—took its place. The next chapter looks at TANF and how it is working. Medicaid, food stamps, and other programs help families with children too.

Other programs help different groups. SSI, or Supplemental Security Income, helps people with disabilities. Social Security is still a "safety net" for many older Americans too.

The "last recourse" government aid is state-funded General Assistance. It helps anyone—with or without children—who meets the need criteria. But not all states have such programs. Plus, they usually give General Assistance for only a few months.

4

The War Over Welfare

Probably no antipoverty program has been as controversial as welfare. Why is welfare such a "hot-button" topic? How well is the current program doing?

Welfare Today

Today, TANF is the primary welfare program. TANF is Temporary Aid for Needy Families. The Personal Responsibility and Work Opportunity Reconciliation Act created TANF in 1996. The Act amended other antipoverty laws too. The 1996 law "mark[ed] the end of federal entitlement to assistance."[1]

As before, most TANF money comes from the federal government. But TANF money now takes the form of block grants to states. States design their own welfare programs. Needy families can then get cash from the state.

But TANF money has strings attached. Families must meet certain conditions. Plus, limits apply.

Financial tests determine who gets TANF. Families must have very low incomes to get cash benefits. Children getting aid must live with a parent. Mothers under eighteen must live with their parents or other "responsible adults."

Of course, the first word in TANF is "temporary." "Welfare should not be a way of life," declared Congress.[2] Most people can get cash for only five years. States can excuse up to 20 percent of their welfare rolls from TANF's time limits. But TANF would cut off the rest when time ran out.

Another change dealt with aliens, or noncitizens. Congress did not want to pay for people who might never have worked in America. Thus, the 1996 changes cut off help for aliens. A 2002 proposal would allow food stamps if someone had lived in the United States for more than five years.

Cash benefits vary from state to state. As of 1998, Mississippi gave the lowest payment for a family of three (one parent and two children): $120 per month. Alaska gave the highest monthly payment: $1,025.[3]

Some differences make sense. Heating bills are higher in Alaska than in Mississippi. Rent generally costs more in Hawaii than in Tennessee. Yet

This mother and child live in the Anacostia neighborhood of Washington, D.C., one of the city's most impoverished neighborhoods. Changes in the antipoverty program known as welfare could have an impact on the lives of many children.

differences are not just the cost of living. They reflect each state's resources and concern for the poor.

The 1996 amendments stressed "Work, Not Welfare." In general, parents getting TANF must take part in training and education programs. They must seek jobs or risk losing aid. "For the first time ever, able-bodied welfare recipients will be required to work for their benefits," said a report from Congress.[4]

TANF works with other programs. Child-care assistance pays for day care while a parent goes to school or works. In some states, this benefit goes on for a year or more after families leave welfare.

Nutrition programs continue during and after TANF. The food stamp program gives eligible people either a plastic card (like many store gift cards) or paper coupons. People can only use them to buy food. Women, Infants and Children (WIC) is another program. Children up to age five, plus pregnant and new mothers, can get vouchers for certain foods, plus nutrition counseling.

Medicaid continues alongside TANF too. Most states still give Medicaid for a year or more after families leave welfare. That way, Medicaid gives some health coverage once parents start jobs.

Shrinking Welfare Rolls

Supporters of TANF had one main goal: Cut the welfare rolls. Taxpayers would save money. Families would grow more independent.

From 1994 to 1999, welfare rolls shrank by half. The reasons given for the reduction varied. The liberal Urban Institute credited a good economy, not welfare reform, with most of the drop. The conservative American Enterprise Institute said that welfare reform caused the decrease. "Welfare Reform Works," announced a 2002 report from President George W. Bush's office.[5] The report noted that welfare rolls shrank even after a minor recession in 2001. (In the past, welfare rolls grew even when the economy did well.)

TANF came before Congress for reauthorization

in 2002 and 2003. That rekindled debate about welfare. That debate still continues today.

Dependency vs. a Safety Net

Welfare gives a "safety net" to families with children. Yet some critics wonder whether America should provide help at all. James Madison once said, "I cannot undertake to lay my finger on that article of the Constitution which granted a right to Congress of expending, on objects of benevolence, the money of their constituents."[6]

The "welfare state" also irks champions of "free enterprise." Without welfare, taxpayers would spend more money on other things. Thus, welfare interferes with people's choices. In theory, that makes the economy less efficient.

Welfare critics also cite Franklin D. Roosevelt's warning:

> Continued dependence upon relief induces a spiritual and moral disintegration fundamentally destructive to the national fiber. To dole out relief in this way is to administer a narcotic, a subtle destroyer of the human spirit. . . . We must preserve not only the bodies of the unemployed from destitution but also their self-respect, their self-reliance and courage and determination.[7]

In other words, critics say, welfare hurts even those it should help. If people become dependent, their self-esteem suffers. People stop trying to better themselves. They miss out on the American dream.

Then there is the bottom line. The more a program

costs, the more people pay for it in taxes. Welfare programs cost over $350 billion per year by the mid-1990s, said former Republican welfare adviser Ron Haskins. Former Democratic adviser Wendell Primus said most of that was for old and disabled people and medical assistance. He figured the amount for welfare families was more like $40 billion a year.[8] Either way, the monetary cost is high.

Of course, other government services cost money too. For example, President Bush's 2004 proposed budget asked for $380 billion for discretionary military spending.[9] How high or low the spending level for any program appears depends on one's relative priorities.

Family Values

The 1996 law said, "Marriage is an essential institution of a successful society which promotes the interests of children."[10] The law noted that the percentage of births that were out of wedlock went up from 10.7 percent in 1970 to 29.5 percent in 1991. It linked out-of-wedlock births with higher rates of welfare dependence, health and learning problems, crime, and other bad effects.

The 1996 welfare law stressed "traditional" family values. The law gave money to states to encourage marriage. Indeed, until at least 2003, states could get "bonuses" if they lowered illegitimacy rates without increasing abortion rates.

Did welfare promote out-of-wedlock births? The percentage of all families with a single mother went from 12 percent in 1970 to 26 percent in 2000. Among the poor, however, families headed by a single woman were half of all families below the poverty thresholds. Among those receiving any aid under TANF, unmarried adults outnumbered married adults by seven to one.[11]

Of course, a correlation does not prove that one thing causes another. One could argue that welfare increases the chances that someone will become a single parent. Or one could say having a single mother raises the risks of being poor.

Statistically speaking, children with two parents

The WIC (Women, Infants, and Children) program has continued under the new welfare laws. It provides nutrition counseling and food vouchers for pregnant women, new mothers, and children.

at home often do better on several scales. But many single parents provide loving, nurturing homes. And many two-parent homes are not safe and stable. Abuse, instability, and other problems can happen in both types of homes. "Marriage for marriage's sake" will not cure poverty.

The *family cap* in some states' programs is another issue. Before TANF, welfare usually gave more money when a baby was born. Amounts ranged from $.80 to $3.50 per day in the 1990s. That did not pay all the costs for an extra child. Yet some people felt welfare mothers had babies to get more money.

Family caps change that. They deny or limit extra money if families have more children while on welfare. In theory, the family cap builds responsibility. It says parents should not have more children if they cannot support them.

New Jersey needed federal approval when it started the first family cap. After 1996, Congress left this issue up to the states. By 1999, about half the states had family caps in their TANF programs.

Do family caps go too far? Sojourner had one son already. She got pregnant three more times while on welfare. Either she and the father had not used contraception, or it had not worked. She had another son, but New Jersey's family cap would not let her get any more money. The next two times she got pregnant, she had abortions.

"The Child Exclusion provision of New Jersey's welfare law punishes the child because the state disapproves of the behavior of the mother," said Sherry

Leiwant of the National Organization for Women (NOW). NOW and the American Civil Liberties Union also said the law interfered with women's rights to have children.[12] The groups lost a federal court challenge to the family cap. They then filed a state court challenge, which was before the New Jersey Supreme Court as of early 2003.

Even under the old AFDC law, most welfare mothers did not have more babies just to get more money. If anything, says Jill Duerr Berrick at the University of California, Berkeley, welfare mothers may have had lower birth rates than other women.

"The family cap is unduly penalizing a lot of families," says Berrick. "Damning the victims under this new system is really quite inappropriate. Right when your income needs rise fairly dramatically, your income is restricted. It's just terribly ill-conceived."[13]

Not Enough

The changes in the welfare law may be getting people off the welfare rolls. That does not necessarily mean people are better off.

One single mother, "Fern," took college courses while getting AFDC. Under the new law, she had to quit school and get a job. The job paid less than Fern could have gotten with a college degree. Fern felt that she was worse off after welfare reform.[14]

Fern is not alone. Various critics say that the new law is swelling the ranks of the working poor. On paper, people make more money with a job than with TANF. Yet they spend more for food, clothing, and transportation. Child care costs a lot too, even with any subsidies.

Effects on children depend on parents' income. A majority of people who leave welfare make more with a job than they did before. Yet many are still poor. Unless parents made at least 5 percent more money, children were no better off after welfare, said one Children's Defense Fund study. The study also found that teens whose families left welfare had some behavior problems. This may have been partly because working parents supervised them less.[15]

Up and Out

TANF's up-and-out attitude may make welfare parents put more effort into getting and keeping jobs. But is a time limit really fair?

"The people who are left in the caseload now are the people with multiple barriers to employment," says Jill Duerr Berrick. "That situation, coupled with the changing economy, is very bad news for those welfare recipients, who are very likely going to face the time clock and the time restriction on aid."[16]

Even before the 1996 changes, half of welfare mothers left within two years. Some got jobs and made too much money to get welfare. Others married, or their children got too old to get welfare. Women who stayed on longer often had medical problems, psychological difficulties, or other trouble keeping a job.

As of early 2003, TANF lets states excuse up to 20 percent of welfare recipients from the five-year limit. That helps many people, but it may not be enough. "I think this 20-percent exemption is going to be far too small to capture all of the people who really do need to use this program for a very long period of time," says Berrick.[17]

People cut off from TANF might get state General Assistance. Not every state has such a program. Plus, there is often a six-month cutoff. Then people may just run out of time and out of luck.

5

Homelessness and Housing Issues

No one knows exactly how many Americans are homeless. Homeless people do not stay in one place. That makes them hard to count. Often the status is temporary, too.

According to estimates by the National Law Center on Homelessness & Poverty, about 3.5 million people are homeless each year.[1] That is just over one percent of America's people. Yet it is still a big number.

Other Americans spend over half their money on housing. That leaves less for food, clothing, health care, and other things. What can be done to help?

Unfair Stereotypes?

Was the city of San Francisco a "regional magnet for the homeless"? That is what Sally Pipes of the Pacific Research Institute said. (This group describes itself as a research organization that champions free enterprise.) San Francisco had spent over $100 million a year in services for about 7,000 homeless people. Some of those people were parents with children. Others were mentally ill. The majority, argued Pipes, were "addicts and drunks."[2] If the city spent less, would its homeless people go away? Or would they just suffer more?

Such stereotypes are unfair, says the National Coalition for the Homeless. Maybe one third of single homeless adults have addiction disorders. Between 20 and 25 percent have other mental illnesses. But over 20 percent of urban homeless people hold jobs. Up to 40 percent are parents and children.[3] (The numbers add up to more than 100 percent because the groups overlap. For example, some homeless parents may suffer from addiction or another mental disorder. Some may have jobs.)

The Census Bureau surveyed homeless shelters in 2000. Over 25 percent of the people there were under age eighteen.[4] In another study, the typical homeless family consisted of a single mother and two or three children with an average age of five.[5]

Some homeless children are not with their parents. They are runaways. Many seek to escape abusive homes. Life is even harder on the streets.

Homelessness is most visible in cities. People pass

Some homeless people keep all their belongings with them in shopping carts or bags. Many homeless people struggle with addiction disorders and other types of mental illness.

panhandlers on the street. They see people sleeping on benches or in doorways. Cities have the most shelters and other facilities to help homeless people.

Rural homeless people are not as visible as those in the city. But they are there. People may sleep at friends' houses or in cars. They may clean up in public restrooms.

In short, homeless people are very different. No "one-size-fits-all" approach can solve their problems.

Schools and Homeless Children

Melanie's school would not let her in for three months. Melanie did not do anything wrong. She just had no permanent address. In any case, Melanie did not want anyone to know she was homeless. Students at the school were cruel to anyone who seemed different.[6]

In contrast to Melanie, Amy did not feel ashamed. All eight hundred students at her school in Phoenix, Arizona, were homeless. School Superintendent Sandra Dowling went on the CBS television show *60 Minutes*. She said the special school worked well. It could deal with homeless children's individual needs.[7]

Others disagree. They say homelessness should not change the way schools teach children. Also, critics say separate schools do not give a good education.

"Their educational attainment is poor, lower than that of children—whether homeless or housed—in mainstream schools," said Luisa Stark of the Phoenix Consortium to End Homelessness. One former student said, "I only began to learn when I went on to a regular school."[8]

In January 2002, Congress amended the McKinney-Vento Act. The law protects homeless children's right to a free public education. Schools now must take all students—with or without homes. And they must teach students in a way that meets their learning needs. Children can stay in the school they went to before becoming homeless, if the parents want. Schools must provide transportation for homeless children. They must also have a special contact person to help them.

Facts and Figures on Homeless Children and Youth

- Approximately 1.35 million children in the United States are homeless every year.

- Children make up one of the largest and fastest growing segments—43%—of the homeless population.

- Homeless children get sick four times as often as children in middle-class families. They go hungry twice as often as other children. They have more mental health problems than other children, but less than one third receive treatment.

- At least 12% of homeless school-aged children are not enrolled in school while they are homeless, and 45% of homeless children do not attend school on a regular basis when they are homeless.

- Homeless children repeat a grade twice as often as other children. 41% of homeless children go to two schools in one year, and 28% go to three or more schools in one year.

- Some homeless children live without their parents or other adults to care for them. The most common reason young people leave home is because of family problems—parental abuse or neglect, addiction of a family member, or money problems. These students have an even harder time finding shelter because they do not have adult supervision.

Source: National Coalition for the Homeless, "Did You Know? Facts and Figures on Homeless Children and Youth," *Kids' Corner: Facts About Homelessness*, 2001, <www.nationalhomeless.org/fmn2001/kidsfacts.html> (March 17, 2003).

Homeless Criminals?

On a chilly February night in 1997, Augustine Betancourt just wanted to get some sleep. He hauled some cardboard into Manhattan's Collect Pond Park and made a tube. Then he crawled inside and fell asleep.

Later that night, Betancourt had a rude awakening. The New York City police arrested him. A city law said no one could leave any box on city streets. They could not build a "shed, building, or other obstruction" either.

Photographing, fingerprinting, and a strip search followed. The police finally let Betancourt go over twenty-four hours later. The district attorney did not press charges. But Betancourt felt angry.

The Urban Justice Center sued the city on Betancourt's behalf. It claimed the city law was unconstitutional. The group said the law was vague and overbroad. It argued that the arrest discriminated against Betancourt because he was homeless. It said the strip search was unconstitutional too.

The federal district court agreed with the last point. The police had no reason to think that Betancourt had weapons or other illegal items. Plus, the case dealt with a minor crime.

The court sided with the city on the rest of the claims. Betancourt had broken the law. "He was not simply occupying a park bench with a few personal items," wrote Judge John Martin in 2000. "Rather, he had erected an obstruction in a public space."[9]

What are the homeless supposed to do? Most

large cities have shelters. They say homeless people can spend the night there.

Some homeless people are mentally ill or addicted. They would have trouble finding a shelter each night. Other homeless people feel shelters are unsafe. Some people dislike shelters and their rules.

Shelter space is not always available either. Plus, shelters are just temporary places to stay. They are not real homes.

Betancourt's case is just one example of cities cracking down on homeless people. Yet everyone needs to sleep, eat, and so on. Critics of city laws say they make it illegal to be homeless. The National Law Center on Homelessness & Poverty and the National Coalition for the Homeless have ranked New York, Atlanta, and San Francisco as America's "meanest" cities. But they were not the only ones with restrictive laws.

In Tucson, Arizona, a law said people could not camp out on city property. Clearwater, Florida, made it illegal to live out of a car. Washington, D.C., said it is a crime to sleep on a park bench.

Cities in Ohio, California, and Indiana passed laws against "abusive solicitation" and "aggressive panhandling." Asking strangers for money near bank machines could be a crime. People with "Will Work for Food" signs could get in trouble too if they stood in the wrong spot.

Not all cases go against the homeless. One court said a Baltimore law against begging was unlawful. The law discriminated against the homeless.

Homeless people had as much right as other people to talk to passersby.

Another court said Miami police could not lawfully arrest people sleeping in public places and destroy their property. At the time, the city had fewer than one thousand shelter spaces. Yet it had six thousand homeless people.[10]

Cities with such laws say they want to protect the cities' quality of life. In other words, they want their cities to be good places to live. They want to promote public health and reduce liability risks. They want to attract tourists too. People enjoying an evening out do not want to be hassled by panhandlers. They do not want to worry whether someone slumped on a park bench is dangerous. They do not want to smell

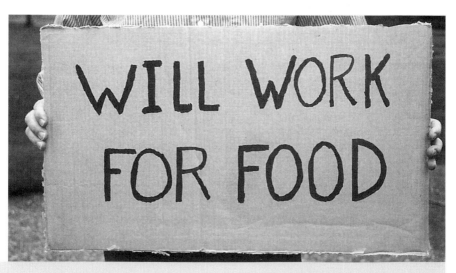

Some communities have made it a crime for homeless people to stand curbside with signs like this. They call such action "aggressive solicitation."

urine or step over bodies while walking to the bus or subway stop.

More Than Shelter and a Meal

At a minimum, homeless people need shelter and food. That is the "bare bones" program in many homeless shelters. Such places solve an immediate problem. They help people survive one more day.

But domestic violence, substance abuse, medical problems, and psychological issues make people more likely to become homeless in the first place. They also make one third of people who finally get homes likely to wind up homeless again. Dealing with those issues can help people get and keep homes.

In Sandusky, Ohio, the Volunteers of America Crossroads program offers a "one-stop shop." Its shelter gives health care, drug and alcohol counseling, and HIV/AIDS education. It teaches money management and helps people get job skills too.

"We provide a good clean environment," Director Susan Reamsnyder said. "Because of this, the residents start feeling better about themselves, and they do what they have to do to break the whole cycle of homelessness."[11]

Homes for the Homeless operates various programs through its American Family Inns in New York. It helps parents get an education. Then they can get jobs. The shelters help homeless children get caught up with schoolwork too. Well over half the students improved their grades.

"A shelter is home to more than one million

children in America today," noted Homes for the Homeless President Ralph Nunez. "If every shelter in every town across America were to replace their temporary way-station mission with the long-term community approach, we would have a much better chance of enabling our children to reach their academic potential."[12]

These programs stand out as models. But some cities cannot even give emergency shelter to all who need it. As of 2001, cities turned away over one third of all the homeless people who needed a temporary place to stay. Families with children got turned down over half the time.

During winter 2002, at least six homeless people died in Washington, D.C. "There is not enough emergency shelter and there is not enough affordable housing, and people are literally dying as a result," said Maria Foscarinis of the National Law Center on Homelessness & Poverty.[13]

Yet advocates for the homeless still see overflow shelters as "Band-Aid solutions." Good wages, affordable housing, and inexpensive health care would solve people's problems more permanently.

As with other political issues, the question is one of economics. Shelters and social programs cost money. That money either has to come from other public programs or from higher taxes. Should the rest of society pay that cost?

To some extent, the question deals with how to use limited funds. It also goes back to people's values. If people think homelessness is beyond a person's control, they are more likely to support programs with many services. If they feel that a person's choices to use drugs or to drop out of school led to their situation, they are less likely to want to help.

Affordable Housing

Some people have no homes because of psychological or medical problems. For other people, the issue is a matter of money. If they could pay rent and a deposit, they would get an apartment. Home ownership would be ideal.

Other people have homes, but they pay most of their money for rent. Both groups need more afford-able housing.

The government defines "affordable housing" based on an area's housing costs and income levels. The U.S. Department of Housing and Urban Development (HUD) says families that pay over 30 percent of yearly income for housing are "cost burdened." They may have trouble paying for food, clothing, medical care, and other items.

As of 1999, HUD reports, 12 million households paid over 50 percent of their yearly incomes for housing. A full 40 percent of "very low-income renters" were in that group. ("Very low-income renters" earn less than half of an area's median income.)[14]

Like other things, housing costs depend on com-petition. The more demand there is, the more renters or buyers are willing to pay for a limited supply of places to live. As a result, housing costs much more in some places than in others.

Also, many areas have fewer low-cost homes than

they once did. Builders act out of self-interest. They want to make a profit. If they can make more money by building in middle-class suburbs than in low-income areas, they will likely do that.

Between 1997 and 1999, affordable housing for very low-income renters fell by 7 percent, or 1.14 million units. The city of Boston needed over thirty thousand new low-cost rental units to deal with its housing problem. Similar problems exist in other cities.[15]

Today, HUD runs several programs to increase affordable housing. Public housing units run by local authorities still offer homes for the poor. Unlike early projects, newer public housing tries not to concentrate poor people all in one place. Many planners like a mix of income levels, including more people who hold jobs. Planners also prefer low-rise buildings or styles that fit in with the neighborhood. They feel that these things lower crime and make people feel more connected to society.

However, cities do not have enough public housing units. In some places, people can stay on waiting lists for over five years.

Vouchers can help people pay rent in privately owned buildings. Vouchers work like coupons. Renters use them toward their rent payments, and landlords get the face value from the government. Instead of living where everyone else is on public assistance, people then have neighbors who work. In theory, that makes the buildings safer too. Yet even with vouchers, many families cannot find suitable housing.

President George W. Bush and HUD Secretary Mel Martinez share a break with fellow volunteers while building a Habitat for Humanity home in Waco, Texas. Such projects involve what is called "sweat equity," as the new owners work with volunteers.

Some HUD programs give grants to state and local governments for low-income housing. Other programs encourage redevelopment of run-down city areas.

HUD also gives money to "sweat equity" programs. These are programs in which the people who benefit put in time and labor to get a home. Habitat for Humanity is a private charity that uses the sweat equity model. Volunteers do most of the work building low-income homes. People who will live in the homes must also work on their houses and pay a reasonable amount.

"President Bush and I firmly believe that opening the door to homeownership to low-income families is the best way to capture the spirit of the American dream," said HUD Secretary Mel Martinez in 2002. "By tripling the funding to this program, thousands more families will be able to realize this dream and join the historic ranks of homeowners across the country."[16]

Despite this, 15 million households do not have the affordable housing they need. Some pay more than 30 percent of their income for rent. Others live in substandard housing. Still others go homeless. Nowhere in the United States could a full-time worker getting minimum wage pay the local rent rates for a two-bedroom apartment.

"For millions of low wage working Americans, even working two full-time jobs won't pay the rent," said the National Low Income Housing Coalition, "because wages are falling farther behind as housing prices skyrocket."[17]

Various lawmakers have pledged to get more affordable housing. HUD has made similar promises. Meanwhile, shortages continue.

6

Help for
Low-Income
Workers

Many people work hard at jobs, yet they have trouble getting by. What can be done to help low-income workers?

A Living Wage

"No one who works for a living should have to live in poverty," said Senator Edward Kennedy.[1] Most people would agree. Yet America has many working poor people.

As of 2002, the federal minimum wage was $5.15 per hour. Suppose someone works forty hours a week for fifty weeks a year at minimum wage. Their annual salary before taxes and withholding would be $10,300. That was more than the 2000 poverty thresholds for one-person households. It fell below all other poverty thresholds. The bottom line? One person getting minimum wage could not meet all of a family's needs.

A survey by America's Second Harvest supports this conclusion. Among people coming to the organization for free food, at least one adult held a job in almost 40 percent of families. Over one quarter of people in the survey said their children sometimes did not get enough to eat.[2]

The National Low Income Housing Coalition has said a household would need an hourly wage of $13.87 to afford the median two-bedroom home in 2000. That would be $27,740 a year—over $10,000 more than the 2000 poverty threshold for a family of four.[3] Should government raise the federal minimum wage again?

As of 2002, Congress had raised the federal minimum wage nineteen times. Though the minimum wage has gone up, its purchasing power has varied. Twenty-five cents in 1938 would buy the same as $3.05 in 2000. The $1.60 minimum wage from 1968 was worth $7.92 in 2000 dollars. That was over 50 percent more than the 2000 level of $5.15.[4]

Senator Kennedy and Representative David Bonoir, both Democrats from Massachusetts, introduced bills to raise the minimum wage in February 2001. They wanted it to go up $1.50 over three years. In 2000, Congress debated but did not pass a

$1.00 per hour increase. The minimum wage will be an issue again in the future.

Raising the minimum wage is no simple matter. On the one hand, workers want a fair wage. On the other hand, higher wages raise employers' costs. Groups on both sides lobby lawmakers. Each argues for its point of view.

Most lawmakers want workers to make enough money. But they do not want to hurt the economy. To make matters worse, predicting what will happen is not easy.

Some companies may be able to accept lower profits. Not all companies could do that and still stay in business. Other companies may want to keep higher profits for shareholders.

Thus, some companies would pass higher costs on to consumers. That would mean higher prices. Prices could also rise due to inflation, as workers have more money to spend. With too much inflation, workers may be no better off than before.

As prices go up,

As of 2002, the federal minimum wage was $5.15 per hour.

fewer consumers may be willing to pay for a product or service. Then employers may need fewer workers. They might cut or combine jobs. Employers might also use automation to cut costs. Then workers may lose jobs.

Employers might also cut back on health insurance, pensions, and other employee benefits. Those issues may not matter to teenagers who work part-time. They matter a lot to full-time adult workers with families. The Small Business Survival Committee says this is one reason why minimum wage hikes are bad public policy.

Groups such as the Economic Policy Institute disagree with such doomsaying. The group said there were more low-wage jobs, not fewer, after the 1996–1997 federal minimum wage hike to $5.15. That was also when the 1996 welfare reform law came into effect.[5]

The Coalition on Human Needs claims a higher minimum wage would help the economy. Low-wage workers would have more money. They would spend more for goods and services. That should spur economic growth.

Meanwhile, notes the group, about 6.9 million workers would fare better. Many of those people would be women and minorities. Those groups historically have earned less than white men. Thus, a minimum wage hike might promote equality.[6]

One could argue that the economy pays people what they are worth. Yet many minimum wage workers provide vital services on which others rely. Day-care workers take care of children while parents

Value of the Federal Minimum Wage, 1938–2000
(in 2000 Dollars Adjusted for Inflation)

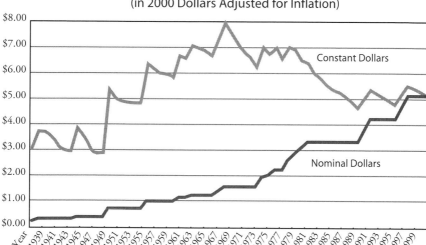

Note: The nominal dollar amount, or face value, of the minimum wage has gone up over time. When adjusted for inflation, however, its value has sometimes gone up and sometimes gone down. This chart compares the face amount of the minimum wage (measured in nominal dollars) over time with its value in constant dollars (adjusted for inlation and indexed to the year 2000).

Source: U.S. Department of Labor, Bureau of Labor Statistics (unpublished data)

work. Cleaning crews literally do the dirty work at businesses, homes, and public places. Food service workers make life easier for people too busy to cook at home. The list goes on. Shouldn't all those people earn enough to live decently?

In theory, the best solution would be to link any minimum wage increase to real economic growth. Yet even that is not a perfect plan. Growth often benefits some parts of the economy more than others. That happened with the computer and high-tech boom of the 1990s. Still, economic growth brings more opportunities. When companies do well, they can pay better wages to workers.

On the other hand, if the world were truly efficient, a growing economy would bring better wages anyway. The real problem is what to do about workers at the bottom of the wage scale when the economy is not growing.

Meaningful Support

Angela worked twenty hours a week at a nursing home. She paid a babysitter $57 per week to care for her three-year-old daughter. New Jersey's TANF program would have paid some of that cost. But the sitter needed state approval. Plus, the sitter's fee would have to be as low as $53.60 for a full forty hours of work. That would be less than half of what she paid her current sitter. "What kind of person's going to be watching my kid for $1.25 an hour?" Angela worried.[7]

Angela is not alone in her worries. Over half the parents in one study said quality and safety of child care was a major concern. Child care costs are a big worry too.

Availability of child care is another issue. Many low-income jobs do not match day-care centers' standard hours. Reliability is another problem. When the sitter cancels, parents face hard choices. If they stay with their children, do they risk losing their jobs?

"We're doing a better job of providing child care subsidies, but we need to do more so that parents can continue to experience a subsidy for a longer period of time as their income rises," stresses Jill Duerr Berrick at the University of California,

Child care arrangements are a big concern for many workers. If a babysitter cancels or a child becomes sick, parents often have to take time off from work; it may even cost them their jobs.

Berkeley. Otherwise, aid drops when parents get even a tiny raise. "Then it's very difficult for them to manage a $300 or $400 child care bill every month when their income has risen by 25 cents an hour."[8]

Health care is another major problem. Families USA says millions of low-income people have no insurance. As of 2001, the group said that a parent of two children who worked full-time at minimum wage made "too much" to get Medicaid in twenty-six states.[9] The other states' programs gave at least some help at that level.

Of course, more help for child care and health care costs money. That money must come either from higher taxes or less spending in other programs. Once again, help for the poor boils down to a budget battle.

Education

In general, the higher one's education level is, the more that person can earn. Improving education can thus reduce poverty. If children can graduate from high school, their lifetime earning power goes up. If those children go to college, their earning ability goes up even more.

To some extent, adults can get more education as part of state welfare programs. As noted earlier, the goal is not to help people get college degrees. Rather, the aim is to let people get a job so they can get off welfare. Critics say such programs should go further. If people could get college degrees, they might actually be able to move up on the income scale. Then they could get off welfare and earn a lot more too.

Education is probably the best way for anyone to improve his or her earning ability. In theory, a better educated population could help raise wages overall. But the present glut of unskilled labor makes this unlikely. That still leaves the question of what to do about the lowest-paid jobs in society. Until that problem is solved, America will still have working poor people.

Tax Time

Taxation raises money to fund government programs. Taxation can also promote policy goals. America's income tax system is *progressive*. This means that people who earn the most pay the highest tax rates. People with lower incomes pay lower rates. Those at the bottom of the economic scale may pay no income tax at all.

Tax shelters are lawful ways to cut taxes on income. Interest on municipal bonds, for instance, is generally exempt from federal income taxation. The federal government taxes long-term capital gains at lower rates than regular income. Homeowners can deduct interest paid on home mortgages. These tax provisions help upper- and middle-income families much more than low-income families.

The Earned Income Tax Credit (EITC) is one tax provision that specifically helps low-income families. Congress first put the EITC in the Internal Revenue Code in 1975. The EITC reduces the amount of federal income tax owed by low-income working individuals and families. The amount depends on income and family size.

In general, both liberals and conservatives like the EITC. It acts as a "carrot" (positive incentive), rather than a "stick" (punishment) to end people's reliance on government aid programs.

"The EITC is one of the best things that the nation has going for itself in the effort to fight poverty," notes Robert Haveman at the University of Wisconsin-Madison. "It rewards work and supports income, all at the same time."[10]

Haveman and others like Jill Berrick would like to see the EITC expanded. By increasing incentives to work, it could help more people escape poverty. On the other hand, a bigger EITC could cut the total tax money collected. Then lawmakers may need to make other budget cuts.

Because EITC works through the tax system, it carries no stigma, or shame. As one Internal Revenue Service ad told eligible people, "You've earned it."

Unfortunately, many people who could claim the EITC do not do so. Paperwork requirements confuse or intimidate them. Making the EITC easier to claim would help. Also, while a lot of workers can get the EITC as part of their paychecks, many wait until their annual returns. More use of the paycheck option could help people meet monthly expenses.

What about other tax measures? In 2001, Congress passed across-the-board cuts in the tax rates for all income levels. The cuts are phasing in over several years.

Many people point to education as one way out of poverty. High school graduates generally have higher earning potential than those who do not complete school.

The tax cuts' goal was, in part, to stimulate the economy. If taxpayers have more money, they could buy more goods and services. That could help boost profits and jobs. Another reason for the cuts was that at the time, the federal budget had a surplus. During his campaign, President George W. Bush argued that taxpayers should keep more of the money they earned.

Democrats argued that the tax cuts helped wealthy people the most. That group was already paying about 90 percent of all income taxes. The amount that they saved would thus be bigger than totals saved by other groups.

On the other hand, people in the lowest tax bracket got the biggest cut in their tax rate. It would drop from 15 to 10 percent. The share of all income taxes paid by that tax bracket would thus get smaller.

In contrast to income taxes, sales taxes are *regressive*. Both rich and poor people pay the same rate. Thus, sales taxes place a relatively bigger burden on people with less ability to pay.

A few states do not have sales taxes. What if all states got rid of sales taxes? Arguably, states could make up lost revenue by raising income taxes. Most states are unlikely to adopt this idea anytime soon.

What about more drastic change? As America's income gap has grown, so have differences in people's total wealth, or accumulated assets.

"One way to reduce the disparities somewhat would be to impose a tax on household wealth (in addition to income)," argues New York University Professor Edward Wolff. "This would lead to a more equitable society." Wolff says that tax could raise $40 billion for social programs. It would put an extra burden on maybe 3 percent of all taxpayers.[11]

Congress seems unlikely to adopt a wealth tax anytime soon. Congress has greatly scaled back the estate tax. That is a tax on wealth held when someone dies. A wealth tax while people were alive would seem to punish them for saving money.

The federal and state governments often amend their tax laws. A major change may not happen. But minor ones might well get consideration.

Besides, thinking about different ideas is useful. While many ideas do not become law, some can and do spark social change.

7

The Bigger Picture

Most of this book has been about how government can deal with poverty. Private charities across America do a lot for the poor too. Plus, poverty is a problem in other places besides America. What does the bigger picture look like?

Soup Kitchens, Shelters, and More

Every weekday morning, a line forms outside Cleveland's West Side Catholic Center. People know they can get a free meal there. They can look through clean, used clothing for something to wear. Or they can just sit down and talk awhile. The center also runs an emergency shelter for women and children.

Across America, private charities give hands-on help to the poor. Some groups help the poor as part of their religious duty. Other groups are nonsectarian. They help the poor as a way to make society better.

The types of help vary greatly. Some organizations give food, shelter, or clothing. Sometimes the help supplements government aid. In other cases, it is the last safety net for people who cannot get government help. An example might be a single man who cannot get Social Security or disability benefits. His time on General Assistance may have run out. Other examples may be families who have no more time left on TANF.

Other groups may give specific services to the poor. A hospital may run a free or low-cost health clinic. A legal aid society may help clients deal with creditors' claims, accident cases, and other legal matters.

Some organizations help poor people get benefits. The Massachusetts Coalition for the Homeless runs a program that helps homeless people get Social Security or disability payments. Poor people may need help filling out the forms. The group also shows poor people how to lobby lawmakers and vote. That way they can have a say in public policy. Another program helps people get furniture, linens, and other things when they finally find a home.

Some groups work as advocates for the poor. Call To Renewal brings together different church groups.

It works to change public policy. For example, the group has said that TANF should be less strict in how it treats poor people. The group also works for racial equality, believing that if people have more opportunities, that can help them get out of poverty.

Other groups promote a variety of programs. The United Way gives money to thousands of groups nationwide. Those groups help the poor, promote health care, improve education, and provide other services.

David Tuerck of Suffolk University estimated that individual giving to charities that help the poor was about $17 billion as of 1996. Another $14 billion of government money went to about eighty-six thousand private groups that help the poor.[1] Clearly, all these efforts add up.

The Debate About Faith-Based Initiatives

Some of the groups that get government money to help the poor are religious. As of 2001, Lutheran Services in America got over $2.7 billion from the government. Catholic Charities got over $1.4 billion. The Salvation Army got over $375,000.[2]

In general, the use of such money must meet certain conditions. Those rules aim to avoid violating the Constitution's guarantee of the separation of church and state. Groups have had to avoid discrimination in whom they hire to work in such programs. They could not just hire members of their own religion. Groups have had to give help to people no matter what religion they were.

In addition, groups could not make people take part in religious activities in order to get help. A cross or Star of David could stay on the wall. But a group could not make someone listen to a sermon before getting a hot meal.

While some large religious groups get government money, many smaller ones do not. Should government give even more money to private religious groups to fight poverty?

In 2001, President George W. Bush issued an Executive Order setting up the White House Office of Faith-Based and Community Initiatives. The president

Many faith-based organizations and other private groups work to help the poor. At a rally held in 2000, the Reverend Emory Searcy called on churches to take action to end poverty.

saw faith-based organizations as "indispensable" in meeting poor people's needs. He wanted such groups to have "the fullest opportunity permitted by law to compete on a level playing field" for government money.[3]

The president said that many faith-based programs work well, especially at the local, grassroots level. He contrasted that with large government programs run by bureaucracies. If a private charity could do the job better, he said, government should support that. Also, Bush argued, "Faith can move people in ways that government can't."[4]

Critics like the American Civil Liberties Union worried. Would support for faith-based groups cross the line between separation of church and state? Relaxing rules about hiring or taking part in religious activities could make it easier for groups to get money. But wanting to help is not a good reason to do something if the Constitution would forbid it.

Too much red tape may also keep small, grassroots groups from getting much government money. One option would be to say religious groups do not have to comply with as many rules. But would tax money then go to substandard programs?

Other arguments look at the overall level of government aid. Helping more groups to help the poor sounds like a good idea. But if total funding for poverty programs stays the same, more groups may just be splitting the same pot of money. America's poor may be no better off than before.

The debate over faith-based initiatives continues. Some people want faith-based groups to have more access to government money. But if funding programs cross constitutional lines, critics may challenge them in court.

No Easy Answers

There are no easy answers to the problem of poverty in America. In a country with great wealth, millions of people still fall short of government-set poverty thresholds. On their own, they do not have enough to meet basic needs. They rely on government help and private groups to make up the shortfall.

Many people debate what kind of help government should give to poor people. What, if anything, should people expect? When does help make people too dependent? Limited resources limit how much government can do.

Other people say the best thing is to stimulate economic growth. The better the economy is, the more jobs there should be. The more people who have jobs, the more likely it is that they can pay for basic needs.

Other people want to beef up education. The number of low-skilled jobs is limited. Plus, those jobs pay far less than many other kinds of work. But people who do not finish high school may not have other options. Thus, dropouts are more likely to be poor than other people.

Some people might say that dropout rates reflect individual decisions and poor people should live with their choices. Other people would say America owes all of its children a good education. Education and skills can help people get out of poverty. They can also help America's young people do more for society when they are adults.

Still other arguments about poverty focus on the family. Statistics show that children with single, never-married mothers are more likely to be poor than other children. Both Democrats and Republicans want fewer teen pregnancies. But people disagree strongly about how this can be done.

Poverty is a persistent problem. America has spent many billions of dollars on programs to help the poor. Yet millions remain in need. Thus, policy makers will continue to debate what America can do about the problem of poverty.

The Global View

This book has looked at poverty in America. Compared to other industrialized countries, the United States has the highest percentage of poor children. America also spends the smallest share of its gross domestic product (GDP) to fight poverty.[5] (The GDP is the value of all goods and services produced in a country.)

On the other hand, as Robert Rector of the Heritage Foundation said in the title of a *Wall Street Journal* editorial, "America Has the World's Richest Poor People."[6] Most poor Americans have clean drinking water. They have a place to live. They get enough food to eat. In some developing countries, most of the people lack even these basics. People struggle every day to survive.

In many parts of the developing world, such as Africa, many people lack such necessities as clean water, adequate food, and health care.

Why does this matter? People want to be humanitarian, or kind. They care what happens to other human beings. All the world's major religions tell their followers to help the poor.

Economics is a reason to help the world's poor too. International trade is complicated. In general, though, the higher other people's standard of living becomes, the more money they have to spend. That raises demand for goods and services. That can lead to more sales to people in those countries. Thus, helping others can promote an economic climate around the world in which everyone benefits.

Politics is another reason for Americans to address world poverty. Global giving adds to good-will toward the United States. It promotes security too. It is argued that people who have nothing are more likely to fall prey to terrorists who want to start a war against the "haves" by the "have-nots."

America must still deal with poverty at home. Meanwhile, it must look at the global picture. After all, America is part of the world. Once again, though, people's values will affect how they want to deal with poverty.

How Can You Make a Difference?

Learn all you can about poverty. Think about what values are most important to you. How do your informed opinions reflect those values?

When you turn eighteen, you will be able to vote. Find out where candidates stand on social issues.

Your vote really can affect America's policies at the national, state, and local levels.

In your personal life, remember that certain factors improve chances for material comfort. They include getting a good education, building family ties, working hard, and avoiding substance abuse. Certainly these are not the only factors. But they are matters you have some control over.

Now is a good time to learn basic money skills. Find out how to balance a checkbook. Make a budget and stick to it. Track your income and expenses.

Whether you are wealthy, poor, or in between, talk with your parents about family finances. You do not need to know all the details. But a general grasp will help you understand your family and its needs better. That information will also help if you want to get financial aid for college.

An old adage says, "Money talks." If you care about addressing poverty, figure out what charitable giving can fit within your budget. Even a small amount gives you a stake in making a difference. This is especially true with local organizations or local chapters of national charities.

When giving to any group, know what its goals are. Ask how much money goes for programs and services. Compare that to how much goes to running the group or raising money. Reputable groups will freely share this information. Call your state attorney general's office if you have any questions.

Get involved in hands-on projects too. You do not need money to help. Plus, hands-on work helps you better understand the problems facing poor people.

Young people, like these teens working on a food drive, can get involved to address the problem of poverty in their own communities.

Seventeen-year-old Laura volunteered with the local chapter of the American Red Cross. She worked on life skills workshops for low-income people. Laura felt the program made a real difference in people's lives.

"Shelters for the homeless and subsidies for people who are unemployed are a great help, but our focus was on teaching people how to find and keep a job, manage their money, or find adequate housing," explains Laura. "It's almost impossible for people to move out of poverty without these basic skills, and too often these are things they haven't learned before."[7]

Chris hoisted a hammer for Habitat for Humanity. Together with other volunteers, he worked Saturday mornings to build a new house. The people who would live there helped too. Chris saw how much owning a home meant to them.

Quinn spent two summers volunteering in rural South Carolina. Her group helped a family get running water for its home and cleared away trash. Volunteers also helped children learn to read. Meanwhile, Quinn saw firsthand the exhaustion and desperation in working poor people's lives.

Volunteering cannot fix everyone's problems. Yet it can change some people's lives. It also gives you insight into social issues. Once you have personally seen the problems facing America's poor, you can never forget them.

Chapter Notes

Chapter 1. Unequal Wealth

1. Aaron Donovan, "Homelessness Is Hidden from Friends at College," *The New York Times*, January 5, 2002, p. B6.

2. Personal knowledge of author.

3. Frank Levy, *The New Dollars and Dreams* (New York: Russell Sage Foundation, 1998), pp. 41–42, 159–162, 188–189.

4. Alan Guttmacher Institute, "Teen Sex and Pregnancy," September 1, 1999, <http://www.agi-usa. org/pubs/fb_teen_sex.html> (September 30, 2002).

5. Susan E. Mayer, *What Money Can't Buy: Family Income and Children's Life Chances* (Cambridge, Mass.: Harvard University Press, 1997), p. 42.

6. Robert Rector, "Welfare Reform: Requiring Work and Rebuilding Marriage," *Issues 2002* (Heritage Foundation, 2002), p. 110, <http://www.heritage.org/ issues/PDF/chapter_8.pdf> (March 16, 2002).

7. Robert Haveman, Ph.D., University of Wisconsin-Madison, e-mail communication to author, September 23, 2002.

8. Telephone interview with Edward J. Welniak, Jr., Chief of the Income Surveys Branch, U.S. Census Bureau, September 24, 2002; U.S. Census Bureau, "Money Income in the United States: 2000," *Current Population Reports*, P60-213 (Washington, D.C.: U.S. Government Printing Office, September 2001), p. 2.

9. Telephone interview with Edward J. Welniak, Jr.

10. U.S. Census Bureau, pp. 7–8.

11. Telephone interview with Edward J. Welniak, Jr.; U.S. Census Bureau, p. 8.

12. Haveman.

13. Louis Lavelle, et al., "Executive Pay," *Business Week Online*, April 16, 2001, <http://www.businessweek.com/magazine/content/01_16/b3728013.htm> (February 10, 2003); United for a Fair Economy, "Executive Excess 2001," August 28, 2001, <http://www.ufenet.org/press/2001/EE2001.pdf> (February 10, 2003); Neal Peirce, "Facing America's Vast Income Gap," *Baltimore Sun*, September 6, 2001, p. 15A.

14. Steve Forbes, "Why the List?" *Forbes Magazine*, October 8, 2001, p. 29, <http://www.forbes.com/forbes/2001/1008/029a.html> (January 9, 2002).

15. Ibid.

Chapter 2. Who Are the Poor?

1. Robert Haveman, Ph.D., University of Wisconsin-Madison, e-mail communication to author, September 23, 2002.

2. Gordon M. Fisher, "The Development and History of the Poverty Thresholds," *Social Security Bulletin*, Spring 1992, p. 43, <http://www.ssa.gov/history/fisheronpoverty.html> (September 23, 2002).

3. Ibid.

4. U.S. Census Bureau, "Poverty in the United States: 2000," *Current Population Reports*, P60-214 (Washington, D.C.: U.S. Government Printing Office, September 2001), p. 5.

5. Ibid., pp. 1–2.

6. Ibid., pp. 2–6.

7. Ibid., p. 2.

8. William Julius Wilson, *When Work Disappears: The World of the New Urban Poor* (New York: Alfred A. Knopf, 1996), pp. 20–21, 51–54.

9. Personal knowledge of author based on donations made by Fairview Park, Ohio, Junior Women's Club, 2000–2002.

10. U.S. Census Bureau, p. 2.

11. Personal interview with youth volunteer Quinn Cassidy, February 25, 2002, and follow-up e-mail, September 25, 2002.

12. Lynn Hulsey and Mei-ling Hopgood, "Off Welfare, But Still in Poverty," *Dayton Daily News*, June 16, 2002, p. 1A.

13. Barbara Ehrenreich, *Nickel and Dimed: On (Not) Getting By in America* (New York: Metropolitan Books, 2001).

14. Jill Duerr Berrick, *Faces of Poverty: Portraits of Women and Children on Welfare* (New York: Oxford University Press, 1995), pp. 43–53.

15. U.S. Census Bureau, "Children with Single Parents—How They Fare," September 1997, <http://www.census.gov/prod/3/97pubs/cb-9701.pdf> (September 26, 2002).

16. National Coalition for the Homeless, "David's Experience," n.d., <http://www.nationalhomeless.org/experiences/david.html> (October 3, 2002).

17. Families USA, "Key Facts on Providing Health Insurance for Newly Unemployed Workers," October 15, 2001, <http://www.familiesusa.org/media/pdf/stimulus.pdf> (February 10, 2003); Sherry Glied, et al., "Bare-Bones Health Plans: Are They Worth the Money?" *Commonwealth Fund*, May 2002, <http://www.cmwf.org/programs/insurance/glied_barebones_ib_518.pdf> (September 25, 2002).

18. Families USA, "Millions of Americans Are Falling Through the Health Care Safety Net," press release, July 19, 2001, <http://www.familiesusa.org/media/press/2001/medicaidholes.htm> (January 17, 2002).

19. National Coalition for the Homeless, "Joann's Experience," n.d., <http://www.nationalhomeless.org/experiences/joann.html> (January 25, 2002).

20. National Alliance for the Mentally Ill, Statement by NAMI Directors, "New Report Shows Costs of Medications for Severe Mental Illnesses Significantly Higher in United States, Than In Europe," press release,

July 15, 1998, <http://www.nami.org/pressroom/980802212813.html> (March 19, 2002).

21. National Alliance for the Mentally Ill, "NAMI Challenges Decision Makers to Make Mental Illness Recovery a Priority," press release, October 1, 1999, <http://www.nami.org/pressroom/991001.html> (March 19, 2002).

22. Steven Greenhouse, "Farm Work by Children Tests Labor Laws," *The New York Times*, August 6, 2000, p. 1.12.

23. Ibid.

24. Families USA, "Prices of Most-Prescribed Drugs for Seniors Rose More than Twice the Rate of Inflation Last Year," press release, June 12, 2001, <http://www.familiesusa.org/media/press/2001/makesick.htm> (March 19, 2002); see also Families USA, "Seniors' Prescription Drug Bills Projected To More Than Double in Next 10 Year[s]," press release, July 2000, <http://www.familiesusa.org/media/press/2000/prdrugod.htm> (March 19, 2002).

25. Susan E. Mayer, *What Money Can't Buy: Family Income and Children's Life Chances* (Cambridge, Mass.: Harvard University Press, 1997), p. 42.

26. Ibid.

27. Ibid., pp. 46–48, 114–120.

28. Arloc Sherman, *Poverty Matters: The Cost of Child Poverty in America* (Washington, D.C.: Children's Defense Fund, 1997), pp. 3–8, 14–19, <http://www.childrensdefense.org/pdf/povmat.pdf> (April 15, 2002).

Chapter 3. What Has America Done About Poverty?

1. Gerald A. Danzer, et al., *The Americans: Reconstruction Through the 20th Century* (Evanston, Ill.: McDougal Littell, Inc., 2002), p. 495.

2. Ibid.

3. Benjamin I. Page and James R. Simmons, *What Government Can Do: Dealing with Poverty and Inequality* (Chicago: University of Chicago Press, 2000), p. 79.

4. U.S. Department of Labor, "Value of the Federal Minimum Wage, 1938–2000," <http://www.dol.gov/dol/esa/public/minwage/chart2.htm> (March 10, 2002).

5. Michael Harrington, *The Other America: Poverty in the United States* (New York: Simon & Schuster Touchstone Books, 1997), pp. 4–17, 190.

6. Danzer, et al., p. 685.

7. House Report No. 104-651, to accompany H.R. 3734, June 27, 1996, in U.S. Code, Congressional, and Administrative News, 104th Congress, Second Session, 1996, v. 5, pp. 2183–2185; see also Mayer, p. 27.

8. Mayer, pp. 26–27.

9. U.S. Census Bureau, "Poverty in the United States: 2000," *Current Population Reports*, P60-214 (Washington, D.C.: U.S. Government Printing Office, September 2001).

10. "Black Woman Indicted for Cheating Welfare System of $355,000," *Jet*, October 14, 1996, p. 56; "Man Charged with Cheating Welfare System; Lived Luxuriously at Trump Tower in Manhattan," *Jet*, October 31, 1994, p. 19; "New York Woman Claimed 73 Kids, Cheated Welfare System Out of Nearly $450,000," *Jet*, June 20, 1994, p. 40.

11. H.R. Rep. No. 104-651, at 3–4, pp. 2184–2185.

12. Ralph Dolgoff and Donald Feldstein, *Understanding Social Welfare* (Needham Heights, Mass.: Allyn and Bacon, 2000), p. 102.

13. Willliam J. Clinton, Statement, 32 Weekly Compilation of Presidential Documents 1487, August 26, 1996, in U.S. Code, Congressional, and Administrative News, 104th Congress, Second Session, 1996, v. 5, pp. 2891–2893.

Chapter 4. The War Over Welfare

1. Department of Health and Human Services,

Administration for Children and Families, "Welfare: Temporary Assistance for Needy Families," September 2001, <http://www.acf.dhhs.gov/news/facts/tanf.html> (February 9, 2002).

2. House Conference Rep. No. 104-275, to accompany H.R. 3734, July 30, 1996, p. 262, in U.S. Code Congressional and Administrative News, 104th Congress, Second Session, 1996, v. 5, pp. 2649, 2650.

3. Agency for Children and Families, "Selected Provisions of State TANF Plans—Part I—(as of June 25, 1998)," June 2000, <http://www.acf.dhhs.gov/programs/ofa/tanft91a.htm> (March 21, 2002).

4. H.R. Rep. No. 104-275, at 262, pp. 2649–2650.

5. Office of the President, "Working Toward Independence," February 2002, p. 5, <http://www.whitehouse.gov/news/releases/2002/02/welfare-reform-announcement-book.pdf> (March 1, 2002).

6. Larry Elder, "The Constitution Versus the Modern Welfare State," July 6, 2001, <http://www.townhall.com/columnists/larryelder/le20010706.shtml> (February 8, 2002).

7. Larry Elder, "Daring to Question the Welfare State," June 30, 2001, <http://www.townhall.com/columnists/larryelder/le20010630.shtml> (February 8, 2002); Michael B. Barkey, "Reviving the Old Consensus," 2001, <http://www.compassionateconservative.cc> (February 8, 2002).

8. Rebecca Blank and Ron Haskins, eds., *The New World of Welfare* (Washington, D.C.: Brookings Institution, 2001), pp. 104, 134.

9. Department of Defense, "Fiscal 2004 Department of Defense Budget Release," February 3, 2003, <http://www.defenselink.mil/news/Feb2003/b02032003_bt044-03.html> (February 11, 2003).

10. Personal Responsibility and Work Opportunity Reconciliation Act of 1996, Public Law 104-193, Sec. 101(2), August 22, 1996.

11. U.S. Census Bureau, "Poverty in the United States: 2000," *Current Population Reports*, P60-214 (Washington, D.C.: U.S. Government Printing Office, September 2001), p. 2, <http://www.census.gov/prod/2001pubs/p60-214.pdf> (September 26, 2002); Department of Health and Human Services, Administration for Children and Families, "Characteristics and Financial Circumstances of TANF Recipients, October 1999–September 2000, Exhibit I," June 26, 2002, <http://www.acf.dhhs.gov/programs/opre/characteristics/fy2000/analysis.htm#family> (February 16, 2003).

12. American Civil Liberties Union, "ACLU Urges NJ Court To Strike 'Family Cap' Provision for Welfare Recipients," press release, August 30, 2000, <http://www.aclu.org/PoorRights/PoorRights.cfm?ID=8096&c=154&Type=s> (February 16, 2003); see also American Civil Liberties Union, "In Legal First, NJ Supreme Court To Consider Law Denying Aid to Children of Families on Welfare," press release, January 21, 2003, <http://www.aclu.org/WomensRights/WomensRights.cfm?ID=11676&c=176&Type=s> (February 16, 2003).

13. Telephone interview with Jill Duerr Berrick, Ph.D., University of California, Berkeley, February 7, 2002; see also Jill Duerr Berrick, *Faces of Poverty: Portraits of Women and Children on Welfare* (New York: Oxford University Press, 1995), p. 15.

14. Randy Albelda, "What Welfare Reform Has Wrought," *Dollars & Sense*, January 1, 1999, p. 15.

15. Arloc Sherman, "How Children Fare in Welfare Experiments Appears to Hinge on Income," Children's Defense Fund, August 22, 2001, <http://www.childrensdefense.org/pdf/fs_wellbeing.pdf> (April 7, 2002); see also Rebecca Blank and Ron Haskins, eds., *The New World of Welfare* (Washington: Brookings Institution, 2001), pp. 103–135.

16. Telephone interview with Jill Duerr Berrick, Ph.D.

17. Ibid.; see also Berrick, *Faces of Poverty*, pp. 16–18.

Chapter 5. Homelessness and Housing Issues

1. National Law Center on Homelessness & Poverty, "HUD McKinney-Vento Homeless Assistance Programs," March 2002, <http://www.nationalhomeless.org/mckinney2001.html> (March 14, 2002); see also U.S. Census Bureau, "Emergency and Transitional Shelter Population: 2000," *Census 2000 Special Reports*, CENSR/01-2, October 2001.

2. Sally Pipes, "Homelessness Cannot Be Spent Out of Existence," *San Francisco Examiner*, February 1, 2002, <http://www.pacificresearch.org/press/com/2002/sfe_02-02-01.html> (February 8, 2002).

3. National Coalition for the Homeless, "Who Is Homeless?" NCH Fact Sheet #3, February 1999, <http://www.nationalhomeless.org/who.html> (February 20, 2002); see also Benjamin I. Page and Hames R. Simmons, *What Government Can Do: Dealing with Poverty and Inequality* (Chicago: University of Chicago Press, 2000), p. 263.

4. U.S. Census Bureau.

5. Ralph Nunez and Cybelle Fox, "A Snapshot of Family Homelessness Across America," *Political Science Quarterly*, Summer 1999, p. 289.

6. "Melanie's Story," National Coalition for the Homeless, n.d., <http://www.nationalhomeless.org/experiences/melanie.html> (January 14, 2002).

7. CBS News, "Putting 3 'R's' Into Homeless," February 23, 2001, <http://www.cbsnews.com/stories/2001/02/23/60minutes/main274176.shtml> (February 4, 2003).

8. Luisa Stark, Phoenix Consortium To End Homelessness, "Educating Homeless Children," Testimony before the House Education and the Workforce Subcommittee on Early Childhood, Youth and Families, September 5, 2000 (accessed through LEXIS/NEXIS, February 12, 2002).

9. *Betancourt* v. *Giuliani*, U.S. District Court, S.D.N.Y, No. 97 Civ. 6748 (JSM), 2000 U.S. Dist. LEXIS

1815 (December 26, 2000), appeal dismissed, Second Circuit Court of Appeals, No. 01-7145, 2002 U.S. App. LEXIS 2434 (February 11, 2002).

10. National Coalition for the Homeless and National Law Center on Homelessness & Poverty, "Advocates Decry Increasing Homeless Civil Rights Violations Nationally," joint press release, January 15, 2002, <http://www.nationalhomeless.org/criminalizationrelease.html> (January 17, 2002); see also National Coalition for the Homeless and National Law Center on Homelessness & Poverty, "Illegal To Be Homeless: The Criminalization of Homelessness in the United States," January 2002, <http://www.nationalhomeless.org/crimreport/CrimMaster.pdf> (February 10, 2003).

11. U.S. Department of Housing and Urban Development, "Best Practice: Volunteers of America Crossroads," 2000, <http://www.hud.gov/bestpractices/2000/best_oh.html> (January 27, 2002).

12. Homes for the Homeless, "Shelter-based After-School Programs Boost Learning Among Homeless Students," press release, January 29, 2002, <http://www.homesforthehomeless.com/news1.html> (October 4, 2002); see also "Homes for the Homeless," n.d., <http://www.homesforthehomeless.com/abouthfh.html> (February 11, 2002).

13. National Law Center on Homelessness & Poverty, "Deaths of Homeless People Rising Nationally as Shelter and Housing Space Fails to Keep Up with Increased Need," press release, February 2002, <http://www.nlchp.org/Press/detail.cfm?PRID=14> (February 20, 2002); see also "Put the Poor Back on the National Agenda," *National Catholic Reporter*, February 22, 2002, p. 20.

14. U.S. Department of Housing and Urban Development, "Affordable Housing: Who Needs Affordable Housing?" January 30, 2002, <http://www.hud.gov/offices/cpd/affordablehousing/index.cfm> (March 26, 2002).

15. Harvard University Office of Community Affairs, "Opportunities for Partnerships in Affordable Housing," 1999, <http://www.news.harvard.edu/community/housing/part1_1.html> (February 16, 2003); see also Ralph Dolgroff and Donald Feldstein, *Understanding Social Welfare*, 5th ed. (Boston: Allyn & Bacon, 2000), pp. 258–259.

16. U.S. Department of Housing and Urban Development, "Martinez Announces Administration Plan To Triple Funding of 'Sweat Equity' Housing Program," press release, January 25, 2002, <http://www.hud.gov/news/release.cfm?content=pr02-015.cfm> (January 27, 2002).

17. National Low Income Housing Coalition, "Disparity Between Rents and Minimum Wage Keeps Growing," press release, October 2, 2001, <http://www.nlihc.org/oor2001/press.htm> (February 17, 2003); see also National Low Income Housing Coalition, "Out of Reach 2001: America's Growing Wage-Rent Disparity," preface, October 2001, <http://www.nlihc.org/oor2001/preface.htm> (February 17, 2003).

Chapter 6. Help for Low-Income Workers

1. Campaign for America's Future, "Fair Wage Superpage," September 24, 1999, <http://www.ourfuture.org/readarticle.asp?ID=512> (April 11, 2002).

2. "Hungry in America," *National Catholic Reporter*, February 15, 2002, p. 3.

3. National Low Income Housing Coalition, "Out of Reach 2001: America's Growing Wage-Rent Disparity," 2001, <http://www.nlihc.org/oor2001/introduction.htm> (February 20, 2002); U.S. Census Bureau, "Poverty in the United States: 2000," *Current Population Reports*, P60-214 (Washington, D.C.: U.S. Government Printing Office, September 2001), p. 5.

4. U.S. Department of Labor, "Fair Labor Standards Act of 1938: Maximum Struggle for a Minimum Wage,"

n.d., <http://www.dol.gov/dol/esa/public/minwage/history.htm> (March 10, 2002).

5. Jared Bernstein and Chauna Brocht, "The Next Step: The New Minimum Wage Proposals and the Old Opposition," Economic Policy Institute Issue Brief #130B, March 8, 2000, <http://epinet.org/Issuebriefs/Ib130b.html> (April 11, 2002).

6. Coalition on Human Needs, "Minimum Wage," January 2003, <http://www.chn.org/pdf/IBminwage.pdf> (February 16, 2003); see also "The Minimum Wage," June 27, 2001, <http://www.chn.org/minimumwage/minwageissuebrief.html> (April 11, 2002).

7. Karen Houppert, "For Her Own Good—With the 'Family Cap,' the State Says to Welfare Moms: No More Babies!" *The Nation*, February 4, 2002, p. 20.

8. Telephone interview with Jill Duerr Berrick, University of California, Berkeley, February 7, 2002.

9. Families USA, "The Health Care Safety Net: Millions of Low-Income People Left Uninsured," July 2001, <http://www.familiesusa.org/media/pdf/holesreport.pdf> (January 17, 2002).

10. Robert Haveman, Ph.D., University of Wisconsin-Madison, e-mail communication to author, September 23, 2002.

11. Edward N. Wolff, New York University, e-mail communication to author, February 11, 2002; see also Edward N. Wolff, *Top Heavy: A Study of the Increasing Inequality of Wealth in America* (New York: Twentieth Century Fund Press, 1995), pp. 51–57.

Chapter 7. The Bigger Picture

1. David G. Tuerck, Suffolk University, Testimony before Senate Labor and Human Resources Committee, Subcommittee on Children and Families, March 26, 1996, <http://www.beaconhill.org/Testimony.html> (September 30, 2002).

2. Mark Silk, "Old Alliance, New Ground Rules," *Washington Post*, February 18, 2001, p. B3; Andrew

Walsh, ed., *Can Charitable Choice Work? Covering Religion's Impact on Urban Affairs and Social Services* (Hartford, Conn.: Trinity College, 2001).

3. George W. Bush, "Executive Order 13198: Establishment of White House Office of Faith-Based and Community Initiatives," January 29, 2001, <http://www.whitehouse.gov/news/releases/2001/01/20010129-2.html> (April 13, 2002).

4. The White House, "President Promotes Faith-Based Initiative," press release, April 11, 2002, <http://www.whitehouse.gov/news/releases/2002/04/20020411-5.html> (April 13, 2002).

5. Sheldon H. Danziger and Robert H. Haveman, *Understanding Poverty* (New York: Russell Sage Foundation, 2001), p. 182.

6. Robert Rector, "America Has the World's Richest Poor People," *Wall Street Journal*, September 24, 1998, p. A18.

7. Laura Meissner, e-mail communication with author, March 27, 2002.

Glossary

absolute poverty—Lacking material resources necessary for a basic level of well-being.

affordable housing—Safe, adequate shelter that costs a reasonable share of family income. Present government guidelines say that level is no more than 30 percent of annual income.

capitalism—A free-market economic system in which people act in their self-interest and compete with limited government interference.

deserving poor—People who lack material goods for reasons beyond their control and who are thus seen by others as worthy objects for charity.

entitlement—Something that someone has a right to expect. Before 1996, people treated welfare as an entitlement program.

family cap—Provision in some state TANF plans that limits additional benefits if families have more children while on welfare.

Gini index—A decimal fraction between 0 and 1 that describes income inequality.

grassroots—Society at the local level, in contrast to its political leadership; the term can also apply to the masses, as opposed to the privileged.

Great Depression—The period between 1929 and World War II when America's economy was at very low levels of production and the country suffered from massive unemployment.

humanitarian—Compassionate and charitable.

income gap, or income inequality—A description of how income is spread out among people.

median—The middle value by rank, or 50th percentile, in a statistical sample.

poverty thresholds—Income figures used by the Census Bureau for counting America's poor people.

progressive—In relation to taxes, putting more of a burden on people who are better able to pay.

regressive—In relation to taxes, putting a relatively bigger burden on people who are less able to pay.

relative poverty—Lacking substantial material resources compared to other people.

stereotype—An oversimplified attitude, judgment, or image of people in a particular group.

underclass—Sometimes called the "culture of poverty"; a collection of social characteristics that occur more frequently among people living in poverty; below or outside the socioeconomic structure that characterizes "mainstream" America.

undeserving poor—People who are deemed by others to be capable of working and/or otherwise responsible for their poverty.

upward mobility—Ability to rise from one socioeconomic level to another.

voucher—Document that works as a coupon so that the person getting it can apply its value toward goods or services.

For More Information

Center for Law and Social Policy
1015 15th Street, N.W., Suite 400
Washington, D.C. 20005
202-906-8000

Children's Defense Fund
25 E Street, N.W.
Washington, D.C. 20001
202-628-8787

Families USA
1334 G Street, N.W.
Washington, D.C. 20005
202-628-3030

The Heritage Foundation
214 Massachusetts Avenue, N.E.
Washington, D.C. 20002
202-546-4400

National Coalition for the Homeless
1012 14th Street, N.W., #600
Washington, D.C. 20005-3471
202-737-6444

**The National Law Center
on Homelessness & Poverty**
1411 K Street, N.W., Suite 1400
Washington, D.C. 20005
202-638-2535

National Low Income Housing Coalition
1012 14th Street, N.W., Suite 610
Washington, D.C. 20005
202-662-1530

Urban Institute
2100 M Street, N.W.
Washington, D.C. 20037
202-261-5709

U.S. Census Bureau
Public Information Office
4700 Silver Hill Road
Suitland, Maryland 20746
301-457-3030

U.S. Department of Housing and Urban Development
451 7th Street, S.W.
Washington, D.C. 20410
202-708-1112

Further Reading

Books

Bowden, Rob. *World Poverty*. Austin, Tex.: Raintree, 2003.

Erlbach, Arlene. *Everything You Need to Know If Your Family Is on Welfare*. New York: Rosen Publishing, 1998.

Garlake, Teresa. *Poverty: Changing Attitudes 1900–2000*. Austin, Tex.: Raintree Steck-Vaughn, 2000.

Gerdes, Louise I. *The Great Depression*. Farmington Hills, Mich.: Greenhaven Press, 2002.

Roleff, Tamara L., ed. *Inner-City Poverty*. Farmington Hills, Mich.: Greenhaven Press, 2002.

Stewart, Gail B. *Homeless Teens*. San Diego: Lucent Books, 1999.

Internet Addresses

U.S. Census Bureau
<http://www.census.gov>

U.S. Department of Health and Human Services: Families and Children
<http://www.hhs.gov/children/index.shtml>

U.S. Department of Housing and Urban Development
<http://www.hud.gov>

Index